Scorpio Rising:
Selected Poems

Books by Richard Katrovas

Poetry
Green Dragons (1983)
Snug Harbor (1986)
The Public Mirror (1990)
The Book of Complaints (1993)
Dithyrambs (1998)
Prague Winter (2004)

Fiction
Prague, USA (1996)
Mystic Pig: A Novel of New Orleans (2001; 2008)

Memoirs
The Republic of Burma Shave (2001)
The Years of Smashing Bricks (2007)

Edited
*Ten Years after the Velvet Revolution: Poetry from the
Czech Republic* (1999)

SCORPIO RISING:
SELECTED POEMS

Richard Katrovas

CARNEGIE MELLON UNIVERSITY PRESS
PITTSBURGH 2011

Acknowledgments

Poems from *Scorpio Rising* first appeared in the following journals:
The Antioch Review, Berkeley Poetry Review, Black Warrior Review, The Columbia Review, Crazyhorse, Denver Quarterly, Great River Review, Indiana Review, The Iowa Review, Kestrel, The Los Angeles Review, Louisiana Literature, Mid-American Review, The Minnesota Review, The Missouri Review, Negative Capability, New England Review, New Letters, New Orleans Review, New Virginia Review, Inc., The North American Review, Open Places, Poetry (Chicago), Poetry East, Poetry Miscellany, Quarterly West, The Seattle Review, Sonora Review, The Southern Poetry Review, Southern Review, Sycamore Review, Telescope, Tendril, Virginia Quarterly Review, Washington Square, Willow Springs.

Poems from *Scorpio Rising* first appeared in the following anthologies:
New American Poets of the 80's (Wampeter Press, 1984), *Strong Measures: Contemporary Poetry in Traditional Forms* (Harper & Row, 1986) , *The Book of Days* (Harper & Row, 1989), *The Best of Crazyhorse* (1990), *New American Poets of the '90s* (Godine, 1992), *Dog Music: Poetry about Dogs* (St. Martin's Griffin, 1994), *Letters to America: American Poetry on Race* (Wayne State University Press, 1995), *Imortelles: Poems of Life and Death by New Southern Writers* (Xavier Review Press , 1996), *Poets of the New Century* (Godine, 2002), *Perfect in Their Art: Poems of Boxing from Homer to Ali* (Southern Illinois University Press, 2004), *The Best of Columbia* (2004), *Under the Rock Umbrella: Contemporary Poets 1951-1977* (Mercer University Press, 2006), *Poetry Daily* (Sourcebook, Inc., 2003), *Bear Flag Republic: Prose Poems & Poetics from California* (Alcatraz Editions, 2008), *Pacific Passages: An Anthology of Surf Writing* (University of Hawai'i Press, 2008).

Poems from *Scorpio Rising* first appeared in the following collections:
Green Dragons (Wesleyan University Press, New Poets Series, 1983), *Snug Harbor* (Wesleyan University Press, 1986), *The Public Mirror* (Wesleyan University Press, 1990), *The Book of Complaints* (Carnegie Mellon University Press, 1993), *Dithyrambs* (Carnegie Mellon University Press, 1998), and *Prague Winter* (Carnegie Mellon University Press, 2004).

I thank the editors, particularly Gerald Costanzo, for his loyalty and decency. I thank the University of Virginia for a Henry Hoyns Fellowship in 1979. I thank the University of New Orleans for two research grants in the 1980s. I thank the Fulbright organization for a grant and a fellowship in 1989. I thank *Crazyhorse* for its 1991 Poetry Award. I thank the Louisiana Endowment for the Humanities for a fellowship in 1993. I thank my esteemed colleagues at Western Michigan University for their support and encouragement.

Book design: Tara Moore

Library of Congress Control Number 2010939574
ISBN 978-0-88748-534-3
Copyright © 2011 by Richard Katrovas
Printed and bound in the United States of America
10   9   8   7   6   5   4   3   2   1

DEDICATION

My darling, this was my life before you
In ragged verses. It was not pretty,
But if the stars determine us my chart
Must wheel upon a vast affection blown
Across the firmament to all you are.
I am Scorpio Rising as from the gray
And dreadful machinations of a life
Without your grace, your great and humble heart.

CONTENTS

III. From *The Public Mirror*, 1990

IV. From *The Book of Complaints*, 1993

I. FROM
GREEN DRAGONS, 1983

Bloomfield, Inc.

My little ones pull
from the ground, hands
cupping their faces like petals,
like shields. Thus they go
wandering, not so blindly
as aimlessly, under several stars,
bumping, turning, robed
in gauze-white gowns.
That is my dream.
In this life, rooted
in the mercy of the State,
they are the flowers of the Commonwealth.
Peroxide, urine, Betadine, Unisalve:
the several scents composing
a single scent that will not wash
from my skin. The coins
I am given to care for them
are diminished in their eyes.
I look into their eyes.
What do they see in my eyes?
Nothing gauche as pity.
I cannot wipe their asses,
lift them in to and out of bed
and pity them.
Not for minimum wage.
Harry, seventeen,
sixty-four-pound quadriplegic,

my *Mr. Non Sequitur*, what do you *mean*,
"I'm a bad angel in God's air force"?
What do you *mean,* "I ain't seen
pussy since pussy seen me"?

When I pull the morning shift
I lift you from the sheets—
your eyes still closed, your
gorged penis pointing to heaven—
Little friend, when you die
I won't weep. I won't even
get drunk. I'll drive
real fast on Rt. 29
and if a full moon's up
I'll cut the lights. Home,
I'll read John Clare's
"I Am" and later on
burst out laughing in the dark.
Harry, some of us are real slow.
Some of us will never get it.
Now, I gather what I can and cannot
hold. The earth's burnt fingers
I hold to my lips and coo into them.
My dreams are prophylactic, small, and soiled.
In one, there is a door I kick and kick,
my arms spilling flowers from the field.
Richard, I say, *Richard, let me in.*

FATHER, I KNOW

that I have changed,
you have changed,
and the spoiled meat
that is my love for you
sways on hooks in a chilled room
of a woman's life

that there is no weather
in hell, only the occasional
sultry voice
of a bureaucrat
shifting like breezes
the fine dust covering everything

that from the *Book of Stars*
we read *no death just*
fall to your knees
and weep and man
to man means swing
your balls in time
with your father,
his father, his father

that long ago a man
and a woman dragged their shadows
from a cave and were blinded
by possibilities, one

of which was to hold
their breath
till they saw stars

that in every stinking closet
a platoon of nightmares
is maneuvering

that from Good Deals
we inherit a legacy of sorrow,
that your children got a good deal,
that from the pebbles
in your shoes you
made a little mound
somewhere isolated and forlorn

that in the *Book of Changes*
there is no hexagram
for the unborn,
for they are divine
and merciless and flock
together onto lakes
that are our eyes
when we are
looking back.

OUR ISLAND

Our father's ship
has entered the mist.
His charmed cargo
will grow precious in the hold
but will never spoil,
salted, as it is, by tears.
He's charted a course
for the birthmark
you have on your back,
I in miniature on my forearm.
Once, dripping from the shower,
laughing, drunk and steaming
in the cold motel room,
he stretched the blue-veined skin
of his scrotum into a map
and showed us the same marking.
I wish him safe passage.
I hope you do, too, Theresa Rene.
I wish him safe passage
from this world of banks and prisons
so he may haul his cargo of outrageous needs
into his own blood and search always
for our island. May he be a hero
unto himself and may you
never forget
that though I do not know
the woman you've become

you were my first lover,
lying upside next to me
so we could tickle each other's feet.
Come here, turn over, I'd whisper,
and in the dirty light from street lamps
illuminating our room
I traced with my best finger
over and over
the coastline of your island
till you slept.

ELEGY FOR MY MOTHER

Eleven years ago I left for good.
The earth has not cracked, or the moon come down
To settle in among the lucid dead.
The fire in your vault drowns out the sound

Of the gentle, screwing motion of the world.
Pitiful nights when caffeine wrecks my nerves
And I waver in the zone where murdered
Children sing, I wonder if that flame deserves

Anything as sumptuous as your body.
From harm to harm, the nights link day to day,
And women pass through my life like water
Washing my body's pent-up seeds away

And on that flowing forth from dark to dark
I navigate according to no star.
I strike a match and watch it burn, finding
In its one act of mercy what we are.

THE MYSTIC PIG

On the balcony of Lafitte in Exile,
on the corner of Bourbon and Dumaine,
at the intersection of Merciful
Embrace and Middle Finger, where Hope's punk,
Desire, taps his cane on the cracked sidewalk,
where I, awed, disgusted, yet wholly
reconciled, must pass each night never daring
to gaze up, the Boys of Summer are doing
the Mystic Pig. It seems they are not always
gentle with one another. It seems they
are forever beating their wings yet never
taking off. In this city, where the mauve
resonance of a summer dusk is just
another flag announcing predilection,
these sons have found sanctuary. They will
go forth upon the packed avenues, seeking
love while shunning the rhetoric of love;
for they have learned to live in a new
language and it is terminal:

Blue flag right hip pocket—*I shall cradle
you for an hour and fill you up with your
father's shadow.*

Brown flag left hip pocket—*I shall humble
myself before you and receive your darkest
blessing.*

Red flag right hip pocket—*I shall salute you*
as you sing your anthem of remorse....

So the passions of men for men are beautifully
reduced, refined, bathed in the blood of the Mystic Pig.

How shall I go forth among these angels,
an interloper to their world,
to them a charter member
of the Brotherhood of Motherfuckers?

I'll go quietly,
gazing neither up nor down
nor left nor right,
keeping their joy, their pain,
their mysterious nobility
on the slow-burning periphery.

STAR BOYS

All the tough dudes
are whistling in the dark.
Wildman Bob's in Chino.
Dirty Dave's doing time
in his daddy's garage.
Wolf's a woman.
Lizard's got nobody.
Now we all know nothing
really happens, boys.
Things just get perpetrated.
Besides, the sun's a pain
when you're tripping
on what's gone down
and I'd rather stick
my finger in the cool moon.
I'd rather sit and watch
purple curls of smoke
flatten on the ceiling
in the black light,
chew on salted scallions,
pop a couple beers
and think a white wall
till fog comes in early morning
and I can go outside,
walk down to the pier
and listen to the birds
and water. But I can't

wait. The stars
are whistling lips
of the dead arranged
as a great tattoo, and if
we could back up, boys,
I mean, right out of the universe,
we'd see it's just an anchor,
a naked body, a pierced heart.

II. FROM
SNUG HARBOR, 1986

SHINE

*We are the degenerate descendants of fathers who in their turn were
degenerate from their forebears.*

Horace

I sear the pettiness
from my brain and go out
among idiot lovers
and sweet zealots of the Quarter.
Wind scrapes plastic over cement,
rousing tucked faces
from chemical slumber.
In my thirty-third year,
quaintly faithless, I grow
more trustworthy, and towards
those I've learned not to trust,
hideously amicable.
If I have suffered anything
of late, it has been
the sweet-sick knowledge
of righteous anger turned absurd.
Yet in the faces of homeless men
I've seen power born to lack of power,
and have shivered
because I know
even a saint may press
fingers gently
to an infant's skull and feel,

for one electrifying second,
an urge to press deeper.
I press deeper
into this dark morning,
turning on Rue Chartes
into the ill-lit Square,
and pause, freeze, gaze
at the cathedral,
wonder why I don't
more often feel it
a strange place for vagrants
to gather in shadowless
calm, and why, passing them
each morning
where they slouch
and grumble by the gate,
I've quickened my pace.
I've judged their lives
as I cannot judge my own,
and my judgment is as
droppings dripping
from the gray spire—luminous,
insignificant. What faith
can they live by, unwashed
and stinking of wine and piss? Faith,
perhaps, that I will toss
some silver chum, or cigarettes.
Perhaps we are made
of stars long dead,

perhaps only words.
I toss all that I am
into the sky,
and old drunks gather
at 5 A.M. in Jackson Square
to watch, to wonder,
to shine a little.

"I Feel"

she says to him
whose face is a dam
to an act his body
seems straining towards.
His jaw stiffens, fingers curl.

"You feel?" he says
to her eyes, which are wet
and swollen, locked to his eyes.
"What do you feel?"
They don't seem to care

that I slouch on my balcony,
as though it is my job
to lean on an iron railing,
shirtless, smoking,
watching the street

like an electric eye
in a convenience store or bank.
She is speechless, taking stock,
no doubt, of what she feels,
and considering *in extremis*

how she will tell what she feels
to this man who strains
against striking her.

I hope she doesn't
tell him what she feels.

Whatever she has done,
it doesn't warrant his
restrained passion,
his noble posturing,
which is utterly absurd.

Besides, whether they can
acknowledge it or not, I
am a part of this,
and I don't want to hear
her tell him what she feels.

I am on her side,
for all the wrong reasons.
But squads of drunk tourists
flicker by, touching things
and singing horribly,

and I know how they feel.
The protean human heart
is nature's crime against us,
and we are nothingness snapping
at its own tail, running

in circles, disturbing the dust.
Let those who would witness
the passions of others
wrap their arms
around the absence

behind the echo
of a woman's voice
at midnight, a voice
asserting to an idiot,
"I feel."

STALKER

He slumps into walls,
into sealed courtyard arches.
Men do not exist for him;
they are the various nothing
escorting laughter's long gowns
out of Antoine's after midnight,
when jelly-yellow lights
of closed boutiques
press mannequin's shadows
to Royal Street sidewalks,
and each little foyer
is occupied by lovers or
nodding drunks or
other men like him.
I and the pigeons are sober,
the pigeons because this
is their hour to fatten
on what tourists have dropped,
to peck at crusted sticks
and napkins stained with condiments,
I because my wife is closing
the bar where she works
and doesn't *need* to see
another drunk tonight.
Black light in shadow,
he strides from a doorframe
when a pale dress whispers by,

assumes her quickening stride
past Fleur de Paris
into the cathedral alley.
When our paths touch
she breathes a plea
for me to walk with her.
I ask her to stand
where the half-moon swabs a wall
chalked over with pet names
and charmed figures,
then step within range
of his breath.
My fingers curl, my knees
bend so slightly
he doesn't notice,
and though I should know
better than to drift,
I imagine him pumping
close-eyed over a public toilet,
feel his dreaming himself
clear-skinned and handsome,
exchanging the cool fire
of movie dialogue
with a *femme fatale*
who finds him irresistible.
He's disgusting.
His face is ripe with zits and his hair is greasy.
His forehead is simian and his black eyes bulge.
All the days of summer stink on his body.

I want to kill him,
knock him to the curb and bang his head
till black clots turn his hair soggy
and his eyes roll back.
I am not thinking of the pain
such ugly half-wits must endure,
how to them the earth is packed
with angels who hate them,
how not weeping for years makes them insane,
how what they feel devours the cheap sentiments
of tactful, lyrical longing,
how this woman's and my fears leech the world's hope,
how pigeons fatten on our garbage,
how so much of what is human turns to garbage.
I hit him once, half-heartedly,
and he reels, touches his mouth, walks away.
The woman and I stand like mannequins,
ridiculously civil in our speech.
Then we shake hands,
like two people who have done good business.

No Angels

A hustler sighs when a large car
slows then speeds away.
Between St. Louis and Ursuline
on Dauphine, gas-lighted stoops
are pedestals at the end of the world.
Young males smoke and wait;
their dyed heads shine
in the anonymous high beams.
This is not what angels do
when they are bored with bliss;
angels swim through the black,
interlocking balconies
of second-story apartments,
diving only to peck the flaked skin
from foreheads of splayed drunks.
These are big, living boys
who calculate the costs of things.
They appreciate leather upholstery
and quality sound systems;
they appreciate diamond pinky rings
and snakeskin boots and license plates
that spell the names of lovers.
They admire throaty hints of hidden guns.
There are bars mainly for them
on Burgundy and Rampart
where they gather unto themselves
to drink and dance. One senses,

passing such places,
that these boys are louder
than they want to be.
One imagines, no doubt wrongly,
that most failed math and science
while scoring well in subjects
pertaining to verbal skills,
though, surely, a good many failed everything.
One wonders about their relation to failure.
One suspects that, privately,
some are deeply religious,
probably Catholic, and that
it is not unlikely a few
have seen photographs of paintings
in which Jesus or some first-class saint
levitates into a swarm of cherubs.
Cadillac Eldorados
from Metairie and Kenner
cruise the market.
Men's secrets are curses on their children's eyes.
Friends and family are a heaven some men must suffer.
One imagines a world devastated by their passion,
forever falling in the back room
of a dark bar on Rampart,
where one boy pecks
with an inky needle
into the smooth cheek of another
a rough little tear.

COOL WAKE

Come on, get your faces out of your hands.
You know, dudes, all this shit won't bring him back.
Let's leave Toothache shaking where he stands.

Which ain't nowhere, which be hollow and all black.
Let's get collected in Lou's garage and sing
Cause Toothache'd dig it if we cooled that shack

With some harmonies stretched out like strings
On fire, some rainbow-layered lonely sound
Sparking like a long fuse hooked to nothing.

The man sang so high he meant to astound
Hard brothers, sisters, record producers
And all them tripping chumps up in Chiggy Town.

Lord made winners and He made some losers,
But He heard the man sing and hung His head.
Let's echo alleys like shadow cruisers

Cause Somewhere's a Nowhere that's got to get fed.

ALLEY FLOWER

Our Lord has forsaken the poor.
Perhaps because the torn, green eaves
on Canal are flapping in the rain,
or because sick Ruthy, filthy sister
of all our alleys and all the flowers
alley shadows swallow, is squatting
over a grated drain, eyes lifted, singing.
Lord, touch her smudged brow
with your dark, leathery palm
and run your dry tongue through her hair;
she counts the starlings pacing
the cathedral tower and blesses
the steam issuing from her body—
blesses this momentary peace
and the sweet angels who even now
are rocketing from the Edge.
Shall we, Lord, measuring this night
against the palpitations
of a cool, urban consciousness,
fetter this sixty-some-odd-year-
old virgin ill-beloved?
Ruthy, no one listens.
Not the polymorphous god you mumble to
on the avenues of twitch;
not the schoolgirls
in their lavender and denim
who trail the scent of forbidden fruit

on Iberville and Royal;
not, darling, even I who would praise your madness.
For to hear you would be to love you
and to love you would be to go to you
and take your hand and lead you to a room.

BLUES' BODY

The souls of drunks bob in the rafters
and a keen, gray glow shimmers the counter.

Fish-faced old man stirs me a cool one
out of what is left of night.

He spins the rocks glass into the air
to glaze it with Pernod, then pours my seventh Sazerac.

Only now, in this light, at this time,
in these states of Louisiana and Inertia

Will Blues' body show itself:
Creole hermaphrodite decked in denim and chiffon.

From the electric-blue dawn she enters,
trolling her wrap over the parquetry.

The bartender rolls his somnolent eyes,
sees, blinks slowly, and turns to the well.

Layering six liqueurs
over a spoon-lip into a double-shot jigger

he says nothing. She turns the *Pousse l'amour*
in the lamplight and is satisfied

then closes her eyes and sips, pinky erect,
the Secret of Life etched on her broad bicep:
Mama love Daddy
but he be dead

Kings' Day, 1984

Tonight, chance feeds thunder to the air.
Couples trot from drink to drink,
song to song, umbrellas,
upturned collars against the rain.
Their laughter, meek, is merciful,
and the dying rain a sheet of mist.

An old drunk lays hands upon a post,
lifts forehead to the stream
running off an iron-lace awning.
I press my forehead
to the cool glass to witness transformation:
someone's son is changing wine to water,

his filthy khakis darken
down the length of one weak leg.
He stumbles on; I fall back into my chair,
regard receding tides of distant thunder,
watch droplets spot and run the blurred panes,
lace my fingers into a child's church and see

three men dressed as women
huddle in the doorway of the Roundup.
Clutching packages, they pass a joint
and wave at cars. One laughs hoarsely
and slaps her thigh, another pretends
that she's insulted. One's fluorescent

fishnet stockings glitter through the yellow-
lighted drizzle when she turns away.
Their cab arrives, and by a trick of light
seems driverless. I imagine they are
bearing gifts to celebrate the birth
of something conceived in a glass beaker.

My friends have gone home.
My wife is sleeping. Tonight,
the cathedrals of Europe are cocked
and ready; the apartment is clean and quiet.
One nervous fool twitching in the dark,
I burn with hope like a star.

THE WAITER

I drift above them,
an angel they glimpse,
my voice the low, intermittent hum
their lives may well depend upon.

I don't want their love,
only their money,
and in this way, too, I
am like any other angel.

Tonight, two newlyweds linger,
so my station is open
well past the hour
of diminishing returns.

Having come late and dallied
over *les escargots*
they finish, just now, the Caesar,
oily croutons in little piles

at the corners of their plates.
By this, and the flourish
of the bifocaled groom
ordering Mouton-Cadet,

I divine their marriage will not last.

Yet when I lift the silver dome
in a gesture of impeccable presentation,
and they stare at what they have come for,
steam rising

to their wonder-filled eyes,
I soften, then carve,
slowly, at the grain, so blood
does not stream from tissue,

and as I place before her
this life of another, and before him
the same, we look,
the three of us at once,

to a gentle rain
dripping from canvas eaves
in that world, outside,
which we fear.

ONE

Let's go, little passion, this room's got grief
And all my books and pens are bored with me.
We'll take a twilight walk and look around.
Come inside, little passion, come inside.

For I have known what other men have known
And, like they, have feared for knowing more.
As shattered nerves prick blood from bloodless thought,
Easing into traffic draws thought from thought

And time felt cools knowing down to nothing.
One dirty pane of glass divides two hearts
Where one's scared that the other's scared of him.
One dirty pane of glass divides the world.

The woman I love is out for a while.
The street, gray baby, sings for you and me.
Find your creaky door to my affections.
Come inside, little passion, come inside.

A Dog and a Boy

Joe Brickhouse saw his dog
get smashed by a garbage truck
in Elizabeth City, North Carolina.
He was twelve and smoked Luckies
and had a glass eye.
I won't tell you about the games of marbles
or how he fucked his sister,
nor shall I discuss in the abstract
his deep-seated contempt for authority
or why he kicked my ass
just because I was his friend and he loved me.
For this is about a dog and a boy
and has virtually nothing to do with Mark Twain
and the rest of American literature.
It's about a garbage truck
that backed up over a beautiful Lab
and a white kid who wrapped his arms
around the dead animal and gasped for air
as his face turned red then bluish,
whose tears streamed
onto the blood-caked fur of the dog,
and who howled and screamed so loud
at gray and porch-lit 5 A.M.
windows all down Merrimac scraped open,
and t-shirts, drawers, scrungy robes
hobbled onto porches
to stare in wonder

at a human being
who had learned so young
how to talk to the dead.

THE BEATING

I will never forget my only beating
at the hands of a stranger, or that you
got down on hands and knees to pound the grass
and scream that I, ten years old, should be a man
and not just lie there pinned, weeping,
breathless with defeat.

I saw an old man push a shopping cart
down Royal Street last night. From his cache
of crushed aluminum and chipped bottles
poked a little brown head with floppy ears
and a black nose. The man, so used to hunger
he'd attained a slow and mournful grace,
paused in neon-blue bar light, then rasped
a chuckle as he gently shoved
the little head back under.

The kid who beat me up became my friend
out of pity, I think. Not because he
ever regretted having sat on my chest
and punched my face until I couldn't see
through the blood, but because after his knuckles
were so sore he had to slide, exhausted,
off my body, you grabbed me by the hair
and lifted me and tore your belt
from its loops and whipped my neck and back and legs.

I am just barely too smart
to blame my intermittent rages
on you and your insane code;
I'm referring to the many times
I've played the insulted ass with officialdom,
the ranting idiot whose "rights"
are violated by some poor jerk
whose soul is violated hourly.
I'll blame them on Brecht,
Nietzsche, Marx, and television.

No, there is another rage
that is akin to a horsefly's bumping
on a pane of glass in late summer,
a wholly unselfconscious rage
we may feel even when
something is gentle with us.

SOMETHING SHORT AND UGLY

Floats across the rug
after 3 A.M. and whiskey.
It got in through the window.

Tonight, I'd like to show
the little bastard how I feel,
how I hurt to see a friend
with wit and grace congeal,

lose confidence and bend
to suck the rising tide
of silence it's come in on.
But all the false and common

sense we bring to matters
of the heart sours in our hearts.
Friend, that squat Republican
who cowers your muse and makes

you feel such guilt for singing
an old tough chant of loving
in a world quite frankly bored
with anything authentic

is crawling up your leg.
Pausing at your navel,
it catches its breath
then climbs onto the table.

Pour the little creep a drink.
Pour you one, too, and me.
It's dark outside, and words
that fly in the dark
mean what they fly.

Put Your Fingers Down My Throat

In the glue of her brain,
an attractive woman, forty-five, fifty, maybe,
has found what she lost in, say, sixty-four,

and inasmuch as she is very drunk
and dressed to kill in leather, lace
and red high heels,

she says, "Fuck it," the way
only a person who's lived can say it,
and squats to the curb

on Bourbon Street, holds
her face in her hands
and shakes her head;

so when I say, "Excuse me,
are you all right? Can I help?"
she looks up through

the web of her hands,
says, "Yeah,
put your fingers down my throat."

I say, "What?"

"Honey, if you wanna help,
get over here
and put your fingers down my throat."

And because it's after midnight
and she looks like she's figured something out
after a long time thinking about it

and just needs to get this
one thing over with so she can
take care of everything, and because

I dreamed last Tuesday that my mother
was alive and making four hundred
a week dancing at Gunga Din's,

and because there are times,
I guess, when a person should feel
like a bad actor in his own bad movie,

I help this woman in her passage
to what I must imagine
will be a better life.

SNUG HARBOR

My friends were dying more slowly than I,
and drinking more, and laughing more,
but the jukebox loved my soul
and my soul was a neon dragon,
on fire in a blue-black haze,
in a book on the history of neon
in a room full of books about books.

Yet my body was with my friends
in a bar we all loved called Snug Harbor,
where the sky through the picture window
took refuge in the bass line of a song,
and our bartender flexed her new tattoo
then told about love and a war,
of a girl turning woman in the arms of a woman
and a man who died in a war.

So each to her snug harbor,
and each to his, the message seemed.

As I sipped clear liquor
and stared out the darkening window
our future did the shell game in Bordeaux-colored clouds,
and our sighs were the contrails to come

or not to come, or come, or not.

Among my friends was one
for whom I fear beyond all knowing.
She felt what song I needed,
so slipped to the jukebox and touched that song.

When I looked at her she knew I needed to walk,
so I finished my drink and moved out
upon the hour of children spilling
from yellow lights of opening doors
into twilight-changing-to-sign-light.

I imagined murmuring tribes
pinched around fires
as first stars opened, one and another,
to form the awesome clusters
by which the future takes no bearing,
and I imagined scampering shadows,
at a distance from those fires,
of quiet nocturnals taking their turn.

I laughed into my ugly, human hands.
I laughed at ancient fears and
my own foolishness
which is my humanity, my imagination,
and all I have in common with the past.

I knew that when one has made a fetish of a thing
and infused its image with terror and love
a soul is born from darkness, and in darkness it remains,
flashing primary, stark colors of neon.

For my life and the lives of my friends
it is the only light issuing from things
almost holy, things
that lie but mean no harm,
inviting us in, always, inviting us in,

the fifty thousand names for night
and the numberless forms which a god
and its consorts might assume
in a world that has come this far
from one wilderness to another.

III. FROM
THE PUBLIC MIRROR,
1990

THE BEAUTIFUL TARGET

Cathedral bells may not ream
the festered gables
of a city night,
but so many interesting things
get blown away at dawn;
so many fascinating folks
who cannot sleep buck up
when bells are skipped across new light.
I am thinking of one psychotic darling
who hustled me for coins
one entire winter of mornings,
of how he'd chat me through predawn
to my bus stop, how once
he'd discoursed on cathedrals,
hypothesizing missiles in their spires,
and that one day soon no bells will sound,
that all over Christendom spires will open
and thin white blooms will rise
upon white stalks and disappear.

My Friends the Pigeons

The American Experiment has entered
yet another critical phase.
My friends the pigeons, who rent
a ledge in the nine hundred block
of Saint Louis, seem painfully aware of this.
I hope I am not merely projecting
my own dread onto them, but if I am
I do so with trepidation,
for pigeons are, by their very nature,
conduits of urban grief, though if
studied with an open, critical mind,
refract anemic sentiments. Oh, sage
pigeons of the nine hundred block
of St. Louis Street! What next?
The Christian Right is gaining force.
The Christians who march with placards
on Bourbon Street . . . will the crowds
cease to laugh at them?
A blight on that day the happy crowds
no longer laugh at them!
A blight on the idiocy of the Christian Right!
I have watched them on television
and shivered with grief.
They are forcing me to embrace
what otherwise I might shun,
such as ugly, mite-infested pigeons,
surrogate angels for those

never told their bodies were evil.
I thank my sweet, dead mother
for never telling me my body was evil,
and for laying a big, dirty feather
on my pillow one Christmas Eve.

THE PUBLIC MIRROR

When I was a kid I froze
before a long Men's Room mirror
and the knowledge that I was nothing special,
that indeed I would never be,
tore God from the sky.

Seconds earlier I'd stood with other males,
young and not, some relieving themselves,
some wetting their hands and posing,
making private checks of their public faces.
They'd left at once through the swinging door.

Others would enter any second:
it was a very busy facility.
I just happened to be there in a lull:
not at all by design had I lingered.
I had decided to wash my hands.

As I'd wrung them under the cool water,
the swinging door thrumped again and again,
and boys and men reentered the halls leading to streets;
I'd thought nothing of their departures until I looked up
at the reflected white urinals and empty stalls,

the paper towel dispenser, and the door
still creaking. I knew any moment a man
or boy would enter and take no notice of me,

would observe himself beside someone who was I.
But that moment I was alone before the public mirror,
ordinary and full of God, God
who never again would stand on the night
looking down at what I was doing,
I who suddenly was a hair more than nothing,
whom I could destroy simply by closing my eyes.

WEASEL'S DICK

A little man, all twitch and turn,
all glitter and blink and rapid talk,
back-waiter in a gaudy dive off Bourbon Street,
he hustled tips and sold bad dope,
worked to play and played to live.

The maître d' teamed us up
so Weasel taught me rules.
For example:

"When da kike yells atcha
juss shuddup or we'll neva git nothin outta da kitchen."

And

"Don't let dat liddle spick jump ya tables."

And

"If ya wanna double-clutch a Visa,
keep a pen dat ain't got no ink . . ."

Saturday nights, when full staff was on,
there were three Richards in tuxedos.
Our maitre d' was not a man for simple solutions.
We were all Dick, all front-waiters
on two-man teams, white faces at the tables,

college boys who talked and smiled
while back-men sweated in kitchen heat
and locked their arms under silver-loaded, steaming trays.

Bobby's Dick got through a month.
Rudy's Dick got canned midsummer.
But even when I was the only Dick,
even at roll call, I was Weasel's Dick.
And it wasn't a bad joke;
no one laughed when he said it.
In fact, everybody seemed to think I was okay
and Weasel was just Weasel, always moving,
looking around, checking things out.

Someday, as two waiters are setting up their station,
revolving from table to table, rubbing silver
and chatting the past as they move,
one may wonder down a list of names
and pause, I hope, at Weasel's Dick.

LOVING TOURISTS

"Daddy's little girl" is staring into the sun.
Her black glasses flash
and her smile is the life of the Republic.
Where they have come from is no concern of mine;
that they are here, though, is my contentment:
I am a proud and dependable payer of local taxes,
a constant consumer of local goods.
I have called the police on numerous occasions
and said little prayers for merchants.
That man whose toupee insults my intelligence
and that young woman who's insulting her own
act as though they have purchased a license
to be silly on a public sidewalk, baby-talking
about sex which, for different reasons,
they're probably too frightened of to enjoy.
He is more than twice her age;
she is staring into the sun.
I am walking slowly, observing them,
wishing safe passage and all the joy
his money can buy. I am walking
the sidewalk on Burgundy,
which in a few hours
will be dark and a little treacherous
when joy turns to thoughtful morbidity
and money, money turns faithless and sardonic.
They deserve each a sweetness—
beyond this clock of judgments—

that compels a quiet
thankfulness upon parting.
But for now, in the sun, their joy
is real enough, his money blind enough,
and she is lovely, her eyes white flame.

THE IMPOSSIBLE

Why must this asking the impossible
precede physical violence?
If I could do what he has ordered
I would be one of God's blessed creations.
Over thirty, I am too old for fights
in public places, or anywhere, even with morons
who slap women and punch waiters.
But now, defender of bleak causes,
I have risen, and he has asked the impossible of me.
Does he wish to watch me do it?
Even if I could, does he really think
I would do it here and now?
The tone of his voice suggests
that he is not speaking figuratively.
He is an angry man desperate for the impossible,
and angry men tell other men to perform eternity.
Doesn't he know that what a man
may do, to himself especially, is limited
by the laws of nature?
There is nothing more percussive
than a man ignorant of the laws of nature;
more ignoble than a man who shatters the calm
of a good restaurant;
more odious than a man who will strike a woman;
more uncivilized than a man who debilitates
a truly professional waiter, and for this
latter transgression alone I have risen

to break this ass's jaw, to see
him sprawled in shattered crystal and spilt béarnaise,
shaking his head and holding his face, wondering
within his slight concussion if in fact
I had done as I'd been told,
and if indeed this is what occurs
to those too close
to those who do eternity.
The waiter holds ice to swollen lips, fills my glass,
proceeds with dignity.
The ass's wife weeps into *pompano en papillote.*
My spouse is not angry, only concerned, a little shaken.
My new friend rises from a squat.
Outside, the parochial night is perfect:
The moon is white and juicy;
the stars, the stars shiver
through a city haze, fucking themselves.

SUNDAY BRUNCH

When I am in a great city, I know that I despair.
                                        D. H. Lawrence

Champaign-hearted for the moment are lost
In steady heat of chummy Pentecost.
Their fingers trim tears from pouchy eyes;
Their sadness waxes as their laughter dies.
It is at such times transitional moods
Change friendliness to shy aversion. Pursued,
A lover's eyes flit, light upon a sleeve.
A likeable acquaintance smiles, then leaves.
Those left stare into smoked-crystal glasses
Until the reckoning silence passes.
Beyond the border of hothouse flowers
Five ragged boys magnify the hours:
One steadies a lens over a small thing
Wriggling on its back; one wraps gray string
Around its quaking haunches; all must gawk
As fur on its belly wilts: each will stalk
Great herds of quivers grazing in his spine
As he feels his spear of ice begin to shine.
When cloud traffic thickens over the sun
The blisters cool; their enterprise is done.
One casually shuffles at the specious sound
Of artful chatter curled loosely around
The stretch and twitter of sweet violin.
A lavender mother, sipping her gin,

Walks slowly beyond melodious whirr
To gaze the grass and trees into a blur
And feel the brackish breeze through gauzy dress.
Therapeutic Sundays relieve her stress.
This world she occupies is so lovely
Submerged in long moments of reverie.

That an ugly boy stands staring at her breasts
Just twenty yards away is minor test
Of her serenity; she will not turn;
This view is hers; she'll let him gape and burn.
But his hand is on his heat, and he jerks
To mock indifference, and this quite works
To shatter condescension, and when he comes
He smiles, then laughs, and her quickened blood drums
Against the dull horror at her wit's end.
That nothing like this has ever happened
Pulses pale wonder through yeast of fury.
She stiffens and stares; he turns, demurely.

Crossed contrails puff like sutured wounds above.
Beyond the hissing trees stacked buildings shove
Against horizon's infinite regress—
The flashed glass mirroring *en face* flashed glass.
He wipes his sticky hands on cruddy jeans.
In the leaves above, a mocking bird preens.
She'll scratch his eyes with long, enameled nails . . .
He'll press and grind until resistance fails . . .

But neither advances; having grown confused,
Both look away, pained, like lovers refused.
Tubercular swans glide fetid water
Where pennies turn green and old men shudder
To see their squat reflections wavering.
Scant yards away two lives are laboring
To gauge the other's spirit's vital form
By how its silent body speaks alarm.
The woman drops her glass and walks away.
The lustless boy measures shimmering sway
Of her hips within the shiny fabric,
How silver threads are made to do a trick
Of light, so that each step casts a ripple.
What he feels and what he does are simple.

Beyond the dips of light within the trees
A pall is spread upon geometries
Of towers; he wonders what a tiny plane
Is pulling on its banner through the rain.
For where he stands all signs are meaningless
As passion, blood and money are to grass
When gross sensation bevels every stare,
And his heart's a private mirror public care
Is mimed before by those who've ceased to feel.
In his miasmic gaze so little's real.
And darlings pay dearly for their leisure
When urban grief seeks pastoral pleasure.

GLORY'S PUNK

Nick Boudreux, sixteen-year-old junior at Jesuit High
School, thinking himself the Antichrist, enters the church to
meditate on his future battle:

"Just cuz I got this urge
to stick my face in the font
and make like a motorboat
don't mean I ain't got class.
Yeah, like, I got a little foreknowledge,
and some pretty good tricks up my sleeve,
but it ain't like the movies
where the Spawn of Satan
can really knock your dog
in the dirt, if you get my drift.
Like, I can give you a headache
or diarrhea, but it takes
almost an hour of some pretty heavy concentration
and you have to figure the Son of Lucifer's
got better things to do, like
getting ready for the Big One,
and that's why I sneak in here
on Wednesday afternoons,
when everybody's playing Bingo
at the cafeteria,
and mess with Jesus
while he's still in his cage,
so to speak.

I had this dream He's gonna
get sprung April 23rd, 1994,
just about when I'm getting
outta Louisiana Tech.
He's coming back as a part-time fireman,
and I think that's some kinda sick joke.
The asshole my human father,
Third Deputy Tax Assessor for Orleans Parish,
and that bitch only nine years older'n me
he calls a wife
will ride their tennis rackets
straight to Hell while I'm snuffing
Glory's punk, him porking
Ninth Ward secretaries and her
going down on anything with a zipper.
When I think on how they
sweet the air with bullshit
at the dinner table, or talk
about the family as a holy thing,
it makes me hungry for the day
I change before their eyes
into what I really am
and chew their eyes out
one by one and laugh to hear
them scream and choke on their own blood.
I don't hate them for the lies they live
but get sick to watch them lie so bad,
with no class or imagination.
Truth is relative, like Father Beecher

says happens in politics when Left
or Right get nudged, dragging the other with it.
I got a B in Civics, so I understand
how two things living to hate each other
are like a marriage made in Hell.
My job's to keep the center
shifting, do the nudging,
and that's easy cuz
I ain't gotta concentrate.
It happens when I dream.
All I gotta do is beat off in Billy's sock,
who thinks he's my little brother,
picturing Kitty Borkins naked,
and get real drowsy and drifty
and just lay there while Kitty
whispers I'm the best, which she'd know I was
if she'd give me a decent chance.
The Son of Man is such a dork,
hanging there like sausage. I piss
on His altar and laugh in His plastic face.
He never got laid neither's the one
thing we got in common. My Church
will be a neon hall with piped-in
rock, where everybody'll get naked
cept for me, who'll stroll
around and pick the girls I like
and take them behind the altar,
while everybody's singing from
books with notes and words

made of little flicks of flame.
I'll kiss and fuck and do
what I want and never get insulted.
If I win
it won't be as bad as everybody thinks
but it won't be no picnic neither.
I just wanna feel something
that ain't got a phony name.
That's all victory is, Mr. Sausage,
cuz to look at you I gotta guess
after a while even beauty sucks."

JEWEL'S

From the gay bar Jewel's
peels a synthetic music, and men
spilt onto the sidewalk
in the spongy Southern night
are formidably happy,
dancing and teasing laughter
from the cracked cement
and black balconies of Decatur.

Suddenly I am perplexed as to how,
emerging from protracted adolescence,
I came to this bazaar, this city,
tethering my fortunes to someone
for whom it is less home than mother.

I stare into the small crowd;
some are very thin, and even in the powdery
light their complexions seem sallow.
How thick is the dread that oppresses
their brows before sleep each dark morning,
and how sharp is the horror
of the light that wakens them?
That their companionable joy
rocks the muted city stars
and convenes the Parliament of Shadow;
that their laughs are as silver beads
from a shattered thermometer;

that they are sometimes cursed for being ill
compels me to pause and shiver slightly

before crossing the street,
not because I fear, or feel disgust,
but because they occupy their quadrant
of sidewalk so unabashedly, leaning
into parked cars, meters, each other
and the door frame of the bar,
swaying and laughing and hugging,
a fierce tribal loyalty
the thesis of their dancing
where once they danced for the sake of dancing.

ED'S GUN

When I stare into the courtyard before dawn,
waiting for the perilous little dogs of early risers
to greet the pigeons, waiting, too,
for drag queens who mope from bars
toward coffee, *beignets,* and gentle conversation
to greet with clicking heels the light that saddens them;

when I stare into the courtyard before dawn,
into the sensual, slick-leaved magnolia
that hangs one limb over the wall
beyond which beauty is truly relative
and danger is not, I hear

my brilliant, illiterate neighbor,
who seems never to sleep, and who owns
a large gun of which he is exceedingly fond.

Lately, he has taken to sitting on his porch
above my porch from midnight until dawn,
talking to the dead wife in his head,
a woman who, according to his former lover
whose broken nose stained our carpet
and whose purple cheeks Betty gently pressed with ice,

blew her brains out eight years ago.
As the story goes, he loved her very much.
As the story goes, he was lying in a hammock

when he heard the blast. I don't know
if the gun whose rapid clicks I hear,
whose silver barrel I see
pointing from his hand when I look up
is the same she'd pointed at her temple.
In the hall of our building he is cheerful.
He doesn't know that I, too, sleep fitfully at times
and must wait for dawn on the back porch,
that I stand below him listening,
questioning his sanity while testing my own.
Last night I heard him tell his dead wife,
"I have enough ammo to kill every faggot in town."

There are no homosexuals in our lovely little courtyard,
only mice and birds. Beyond the wall
there are many homosexuals, and some of them
face grave danger from a man named Edward
who holds a dead wife in his head
and a large gun in his hand,
late at night when homosexuals
are most numerous in the streets
and least inclined to hide their predilections.
Ed's former lover said he beat her
because he couldn't "get it up."
She told us "he's into weird sex,"
and began to explain.

As I stare into the courtyard before dawn,
waiting for light to bring mockingbirds

and jays to the Japanese magnolia;
waiting, too, for street sweepers, supply trucks
and tourist-hustling mule-drawn buggies
to liven the narrow, sticky street,
I am renewed for her who lies within,

and hear Oedipus weeping bloody tears,
and a homosexual Nazarene imploring his invisible father.

ELEGY FOR JOHN VAN VLECK

I think whatever I shall meet on the road I shall like,
And whoever beholds me shall like me . . .

                                        Whitman

A mirror spreads the length of the Chart House bar,
and many nights I have glimpsed myself
chatting with one or another acquaintance,
or talking across the garnish tins to my wife

as she loads her tray for another trip
around the patio of weekend lovers.

It's a little startling to see myself
being casual among others, so I become
self-consciously casual, though I realize
I am but one of several in a row
being self-consciously casual, each
glimpsing how he uses his cigarette
to embellish a rhetorical point, or how
she tilts her head just so to seem more thoughtful.

To be a proper fool among fools
one must achieve the eye of a dancer.
I come to sit and wait for Betty
to give last call, count her bank,
punch out. I sip a beer at the bar
with those who have been drinking all night.

Their infatuation with themselves is forgivable;
mine is not. The mirror in the antique bar
is tinted such that the skin's flaws
do not show, and we are all a little lovelier
for its being tinted, and for
the low, yellow light.

John Van Vleck, thirty-nine-year-old waiter,
would drink at the bar when his shift was over.
I gathered from months of half-listening
that's he'd wandered through the Chart House chain,
from La Jolla to Boston, Nags Head, finally here.
A pink-faced alcoholic, he read trashy paperbacks,
carried one everywhere, and fancied himself a poet.
He tried to talk to me but I blew him off.
He talked loud and said stupid things.
He lingered through last call with lingering drunks,
the kind bartenders must steady towards the door
at closing, and recited his jangling little horrors
and extolled the virtues of Harold Robbins.

John Van Vleck, to whom I never spoke a kind word,
you were not bad looking, but women suffered
your come-ons and flicked you away. Only
the drunkest old men would let you talk
bad books into their nodding faces, only
the youngest dishwashers and busboys would go out

drinking with you after the restaurant closed,
only the mirror cared about your ridiculous musings
on the egocentric predicament. And your poems,
your poems were the soulful prattle
of someone who'd read little poetry.

John Van Vleck, Whitman would have liked you.
He could not condescend to good-hearted fools
who loved the sound of their own voices.
He'd have put his arm around your shoulder
in such a way that neither you nor he
would have known what that gesture really meant for him.
He'd have listened as only saints listen
to the garbled speech of excited innocence,
not hearing your words, but your body's pure motives.

Your recitations seemed always to begin,
"Love is like . . ." as though you could
say sweetly what Archilochos spat in rage
or with Burns tether feeling to a flower.
Perhaps the body itself is a mirror,
and when it is positioned before a reflecting surface
a soul explodes into infinite regression.

The chilly purity of cathedral bells
imbues the heart with reticence
and blows a swirl of feathers round the Square.
Yet scraps of trash sail the morning shadows,
each piloted by a little god

that reads not charts or stars, but stares
upon a flat, black surface that is mercy.

To live in New Orleans, where the dead
are kept above ground, is to reconsider,
daily, as one passes in one's car
the crumbling communities of dead,
the holiness of closure. Lucky dead
in their little apartments watch television.
The marble angels are beautiful aerials
receiving lives as they should have been,
as they were dreamed.

The ideal life is episodic, patterned, heroic and simple.
In the ideal life there are no mirrors,
only goodness greeting goodness,
everything deliciously fucked by God.

There was a time when the new dead
rode on floodwaters to greet their progeny,
sifted up through the marshy soil
and drifted supine in wooden boxes
past homes and storefronts,
down streets at night in parades of debris
as the living are carried through these same streets
by rituals as diffuse as summer floods and television.

John Van Vleck, you shopped in used-bookstores
guided by an unschooled fancy; true genius

may be guided by an unschooled fancy,
though first it must suffer. . . .

How can I know what it must suffer?

Whitman suffered the Old Testament,
suffered Emerson's self-righteous erudition,
suffered the fevered brows of dying boys,
suffered the sweet spray of light
that is a true lover's madness
and true singer's only food for song.
But songs rot; judgments rot.

I saw you only once somewhere other than the bar.
Sipping coffee in La Marquise, you sat cross-legged,
reading a book about Uri Geller,
a man who would bend things with his mind.
Your forehead was wrinkled; your lips moved.

I see the old sick poet rocking a little
and staring, a grungy afghan tucked over his lap,
his white beard pure smoke, his white hair pure smoke,
his life crumbling like stale cake, his sour, sexy heart
            my birthright, John, and yours.

Timeless Love

Not so, (quod I) let baser things devize
To dy in dust, but you shall live by fame:
My verse your vertues rare shall eternize,
And in the hevens wryte your glorious name.

Spenser

I pass the houses of the dead,
The squat huts where scheming ceases,
And slow a moment to regard
A ragged breach, strewn jagged pieces—
Faded brick and pale, flecked plaster.
Our fleet police have cordoned off
With ropes and flags the small disaster.
In humid weather things get soft. . . .
Three weeks a portal onto death,
This brief pedestrians' obstacle
Speaks volumes of our city's health.
A bleating tourist might recall
That here death seemed poorly funded,
That ruin was our fatal charm.
Young men from projects are dreaded
Engines on narrow streets of harm.
The holiness of closure sours
In their hearts and mouths. Emerald glass,
Refracting pain in blacked-out hours
Of dull fury that will not pass,
Is fuming shattered blooms along

Margins of the cemetery.
What civic boss allowed this wrong?
Whose quaint blueprint deigned to marry
Low-rent housing to no-rent housing?
This block of death is citadel
Of static passion, of rousing,
Crumbling quiet that we must sell
In packaged deals of ambience.
The tourist buses slow, then grind
Hoarse gears through spurts of gray exhaust
To ogle the next exotic find.
I stand and stare at weed-cracked tombs.
"Luv suks" in black spray paint relays
A message to our time: small rooms
Beget rough thoughts, I muse . . . then gaze
Deeper, straddle the flagged line
And cross the breach so I may see
What is printed in tiny, fine
Rows beneath the scrawl. Gingerly
I enter, touch the tomb, and read
The tender, misspelled evocation
Of a young man too shy to plead
His case to her he "luvs"; the sun
Splays out a shadow on the wall.
Destroying kingdoms in my brain,
I turn my back on light and troll
My midday dimness through a rain
Of dust a tractor-truck bequeaths
The air. The air is thick and damp;

I sweat, stare up and count my breaths
As traffic thrumps towards freeway ramps.
Tourbillion thoughts will blow away
Cheap sentiments, and mark a course
From where true sweetness cannot stray.
All timeless love is *tour de force*.
Somewhere, a girl near womanhood
Is truly loved but does not know
Yet I shouldn't wonder if some good
Would come to her if he could show,
Who truly loves, his love with words
More fit for loving eyes, not mine.
I'm struck how ignorance rewards
The innocent with loves that shine.
There is a timeless music where
Young men broach death on lampless streets
And on bright days are traces there
Of how a battered life retreats
Into drugged and feckless wonder.
This city's resident tourist,
Peripatetic foreigner,
I wear my care upon my wrist
And feel in nervous increments.
For him who scratched his love on death
I sing brief praise as evidence
Of what soft rains will rinse from breath,
Though rougher rains may burn from sight
All signs but those gouged deep in stone.
So star-flung birds crackle in the night

With messages that click and drone.
Dyspeptic clutter of reeling flames
Squeals nonsense through a nothingness,
And few lovers would etch their names
In that archive of loneliness.
Such love tapers, like fiery feather,
At point where air is meant to part,
Or spirals, burning, through brain's weather,
Mere pyrotechnic of the heart.
Most loves declare for all to read,
But not so they who quiet sing
Into themselves for those they need:
"i luv u more then any thing."

IV. FROM
THE BOOK OF
COMPLAINTS, 1993

THE BRIDGE OF INTELLECTUALS

If Crane had been a Czech, and deigned to live
Till '53, he might have more than praised
A bridge, for in that year of Stalin's death,
Artists and intellectuals of Prague—
But only those the Party had to fix
After an "elegant coup" in '48—
Finished their bridge across the Vltava.

Each morning did they bring their lunch in bags?
Did they bitch and curse and clown around behind
The foremen's backs? Were there foremen? Or did
Each man (were there women?) pull his weight
Unprodded by the ethos of his class?
Of eleven bridges down the spine of Prague
It stands the shabbiest and least necessary.
From the road leaving town one sees the tufts
Of grass and weeds muscling through the rusted
Transoms that trains, some say, must rarely cross,
And notes the webbed faults in the dark concrete
Of columns lifting from the water like
Wet khaki pant legs of old fishermen.
To those whose ambitions for bourgeois fame
Got them torn from their tasks to labor here,
Is there ironic consolation that,
As work is a matter of identity,
So many praised workers remain unnamed?

Anonymous bones of generations lie
The snaking length of China's ancient shyness;
Unknown apprentices applied the strokes
That smeared celestial radiance onto cheeks
Of lesser angels in the master works.

The petty, silly little men who snapped
The blossom of a generation from
Its living vine have watched their own bridge crumble,
And even as this bad joke stands unused,
Dilapidated on the edge of town,
Perhaps its "rehabilitated" builders—
Most dead by now, though some, no doubt, at work,
Scattered throughout Prague, in little flats, alone—
Feel vindicated in their bitterness,
If bitterness survives absurdity.

I'd like to know that once or twice a year
An old man, whose hands are soft from idle thought,
Comes, by bus or car, to gaze a while
And simply marvel that the thing still stands.

"Socialism with a Human Face"

Several times those dizzying weeks
I wondered aloud if "socialism
with a human face" were not still more
than the sentiment of Dubcek's
wounded generation. One young Czech laughed;
"Socialism doesn't work. Our lives are proof!"

The day after Martin Smid got martyred
only to reappear beaten but alive,
no one knew that tanks and troops would not roll in.
Obcansky Forum, Havel as its heart,
was coalescing in the chants
of the disenfranchised "masses."

In the streets after rallies, a calm mulling
persisted into night, and the Square flickered
where students kept their vigil. I observed them
gathered close, wrapped in blankets, sipping hot drinks
brought by friends, their faces sweetened by
ten thousand candles, and considered
that their lives might never be so pure again.

AFTER FRANK ZAPPA'S VISIT TO THE CASTLE

One may imagine him saying to Zappa,
"I've been a fan since 'Weasels Rip My Flesh.'"
Yet to know he loves his beer and music,
Or that years ago he soldered a crazy
Ionesco to his own Bohemian heart,
Does not prepare the credulous outsider
For Havel, designer of chic uniforms!

Less than one year out of prison, newly
Ascended to the bloodless seat of power,
He looked, it seems, upon his Color Guard
And was, if not offended, deeply bothered
By the cut colors of what they wore,
And so sat down with pen and drafting paper
And sketched out how the uniform should drape
The smart, svelte soldier, and in what hues of blue.

Bohemians, Moravians, and Slovaks
Have rarely marshaled martial acumen.
To see them marching on the Castle grounds,
Ceremoniously grave, one might affirm,
Though, the prerogative of small nations
To strut absurdly through the rituals
Of masculine identity and pride.

There is a quiet courage of irony
Which visits the great lovers in a world

Antithetical to their dreams of peace,
And no matter his crimes, each prisoner
Must know his world by walls and uniforms.
It's not unlikely a troop of Sea Scouts
From Bangor, Maine, or Fresno, California,
Would whip the Czecholslovak Color Guard,
Yet what mother of invention would not squeal
To see her boy decked out by a president?

ST. VITUS

In the great Gothic Cathedral of Prague—
Designed, of course, to scare shit out of peasants,
And so parlay a huge and abstract doom
Into incontrovertible power—
I strolled, nine months after the gentle purge.

A god who dices with the universe
Surely will not care for such drab splendor,
But there it stood, dank, crusted with relics,
Neither museum nor sanctuary.

The Holy Roman Empire once murmured there,
And Charles IV is kept in the huge cellar.
I bought a ticket and slumped down the steps
With the other tourists, mostly Germans.

Raised in a nation obsessed with beginnings,
I could not stipulate resolution
As the measure of gross identity.
In the foundation of St. Vitus,
Large, dirty walls of granite shoulder death,
And I imagined kids through the centuries
Screwing in the hollow pockets of rock,

Sneaking down, wicked, sweet, full of guilt
Yet drawn inexorably to the cool places
Near the crypts of kings and bishops, as though
Passion justifies what passion hastens.

WEEKEND

A broad zone from southern Poland
through central-south Moravia
is dying of chemical blight, and no randy hopes
of revolutions or common markets
will make it once more lush and vital.
Eight months after the "people's triumph"
I'd returned to see my child be born.
Swollen to her eighth month, my child's
strong mother hiked with me five K's
to the Polish border, all the while
quizzing: *strom . . . kytička . . . zelený . . .*
Our child, she insisted, will speak Czech,
will have a Czech identity.
She paused often to pluck berries,
and spoke with humor of her parents,
divorced for years, still hunting mushrooms
in the same frail woods outside of Prague:
"They live the same lives, do the same things.
One wonders why they separated."
Blight is a matter of degree,
of course, and that ancient forest
of her country was still attractive;
indeed, the sick rains had so thinned it out
it appeared more lovely for all
the delicate angles of fallen trunks,
and for patches of clearing where
stunted shrubs carpeted the ground.

THE BOOK OF COMPLAINTS

for Pavel Šrut

1.

I was told that most
Establishments kept
A book of complaints
For the sour stories
Of the poorly served,
The principle being
Familiar to patrons
Here in the rich West:
The customer is right,
Always, and as such
May stride like a god
Through a world of aisles,
Touching and choosing.
But the customer
Was, more precisely,
A mere citizen,
A consuming unit
Suffering to shuffle
Through too many lines
Toward barely stocked shelves.
And when she complained
It was to her shoes
As she queued for fruit,

Or to the wall by
The kitchen sink as
She emptied of cans
The plastic bag she'd
Kept stashed in her purse,
Then to the coal-grayed
Sky of sumptuous Prague
As she stood at the
Window, in autumn,
A righteous restraint
Withering within her.

2.

I stood among them,
Dumb emissary
Of good intentions,
And listened to their
Chants and studied their
Faces. The autumn
Sky would turn to ash
Each afternoon in
Wenceslas Square as
The bold crowds swelled, and
The peeved old men in
The Castle got grimmer.

"Dominika, what
is he saying now?"
I would ask again
And again, and my
Patient friend would pause
To translate the blared
Complaints of that hour's
Representative,
Explaining nuance
And brief history.
"Richard, you just don't
know what it's like to
Live under such liars,"
She said, applauding
Another public
Sentiment of rage,
Applauding her youth
And "socialism
With a human face"
(at least the idea).
The night that Jakes
Shuffled from power,
A fine rain drizzled
And kids piled into
Cars and hammered horns
And swished Czech flags, and
The faces on trams,
Even of the old,
In that gold light shined

With contentment;
The Book of Complaints
Seemed, for the moment,
Finished.

3.

          but it is
Never done; like hair
It lengthens after
Death as head skin shrinks
And turns to leather.

Dominika, dear
One, beautiful and
Bright, everywhere sour
Heads, having spent youth
Seeking a cure for
Fear of death, find in
The death of passion
A bitter solace.
Benevolent, some
Would save the whole world
From the body's will,
That half-remembered
Dance of the fetus
Whose dazzling finish
Is each body's first

Wailing entry in
The Book of Complaints.

The privileging of
Mediocrity
Is a sin far worse
Than the fratricide
It always inspires.
Dull fathers pull long
Faces for the young,
Who are not amused,
Though learning to laugh
With one's whole body
Is the first stage of
A righteous slaying.

Where, before, people
Laughed bitterly and
To themselves, or in
Small, muted clutches
Sucking cigarettes
And quaffing rich beer,
From mid-November
To mid-December
They laughed openly
And infectiously.
It is wonderful
To hear such laughter:
A revolution

Of laughter often
It seemed, and Kafka,
Squinting up from his
Own Book of Complaints
In a cramped chamber
Of a gray heaven,
Surely felt the bliss
Of vindication.

4.

When poor Martin Smid,
The revolution's
Martyr for a day—
His purpled, swollen
Face a flag of harm—
Was thrust on TV
To prove that he lived,
That riot police
Had not quite killed him
(As though the thousands
Swarming his shrine of
A thousand candles
Would casually scatter
At proof that he lived),
Fact withered beneath
The putrid fictions
Of twenty-one years,

And though it no doubt
Hurt his face to laugh,
One can only hope
Smid saw the noble
Purpose of his death,
And managed to smile.

5.

From the Charles Bridge at
Night the Castle shines
In golden floodlights
Of ambiguous
Glory. Bohemians
Stroll the quiet dark,
To my eyes passive,
Sighingly pliant.
Yet I am humbled
By the memory
Of a dour people
Opening their lives
To the world and to
Themselves, and chanting
The essential truths
Inscribed there, in blood.

To the Old Town Square
The tourists will flock

And yawn up stiff-necked
And still beneath the
Astronomical Clock,
Waiting for little
Dolls of painted wood
To spin in their slots,
Pirouetting robots
Chiming the hour.
Each time I return,
A tablet of Czech
undesolved on my tongue,
I'll stand in the Jewish
Cemetery, among
The shuffled, tilting,
Gray, smooth, weathered slabs—
Jews buried ten-deep
Signified by mounds—
And think of Loew
Inserting the scroll
In his golem's mouth.

On most ragged slabs
Are pebbles, each speck
A token, a prayer,
A petrified flower
For the laughing dead.

The revelation,
At first, seems simple:

A "state" is only
The page on which one
Inscribes her most bitter,
Consistent complaints,
A page filled with ire
Scribbled in various
Hands, signed boldly, or
Left anonymous.
We are the mounting
Tallies of each her
Discontentedness,
And desire, the un-
Inscribable, gets
Confounded in the
Act of complaining.

6.

I regard a world
That is beautiful
And rank, and couch what
I see in language
That is palpable
And rude, for nothing
Marked in the cool light
Of managerial
Regard survives its
Last bitter affront

To the gaseous sky
Or sooty windows,
And my heart's complaints
I mean to survive
Unto the sweet eyes
Of those I have loved
And would wish to love.

Amid the almost
Funny tilting slabs—
That cram-packed ghetto
Of Prague's lost lovers
Tilting as a field
Of flowers is ruffled
Unevenly by
A randy, swirling,
Dank autumnal breeze—
I will bitch a prayer
For Loew's loveless
Automaton, and
For each hovering soul
Among the muted,
Rain-smoothed, pebble-crowned
Black headstones, and bitch
Prayers for the new life
Of Prague, pristine page
Onto which real lives
Will be written, one
Complaint at a time.

A Brief History of Your Conception

(Composed on the day of your birth in Prague, August 29, 1990)

I recall the commercials for Radio Free Europe when I was ten, residing in public housing in Norfolk, Virginia. Checkosowhatchamacallit sounded like a terrible place to live, worse, even, than Newport News. The word looked like a disease, and being behind the "iron curtain" had to resemble being in an "iron lung."

When I was fifteen I heard on Armed Forces Radio that Russia had invaded it. My adoptive father, really my uncle by marriage, was sweeping mines off the coast of Vietnam, and I was a pain in the ass of Sasebo, Japan. Cherry blossoms littered my path to the bars downtown.

Last summer I met your mother. She was beautiful and funny and very bright. So, though married to another, I contrived to go to the country whose name looked like a disease, to the city Russia had quieted. This past autumn, I stood in crowds of people taking themselves just seriously enough.

There are no pure motives even unto death; my beckoning you forth from ignorance was that I might pardon myself, but you are more potent than forgiveness. The day preceding the night you were conceived I passed through a gauntlet of saints, kings, and angels on Charles Bridge; their stone eyes seemed curious, or malicious, and their heroic postures but propaganda for paradise. Tourist of a gentle revolution, I was as taken with the dashed-off slogans taped to subway columns as with such permanent emblems of "national identity."

That night, between the sheets of energy and artifice, you were conceived. My darling, my tiny Bohemian, someday we will toss gray Czech bread to the filthy swans of the Vltava, and you will laugh at my bad Czech grammar. Or a thousand sorrows will darken the sky with slow wings, and I will write your name in salt. Ema, the world is enormous. Pity it, and love accordingly.

Black English

How to say the distance, not the difference,
is the problem.
In her freshman composition
Shellanda writes that most men
treat cars better than they treat women,
describes her brother rubbing
wax for hours
into red-washed steel and blinding chrome.

She is hilarious and tactful implying
the absurdity of his erotic care, and suggesting
he loves women only in his dreams.

I imagine Shellanda's brother cruising
St. Charles on a Friday night, easing
his machine past the homes of wealthy whites.
There is no bitterness in his face, no wonder,
only the self-satisfaction of a young man
who keeps what he owns looking nice.

Maybe at home he's one mean bastard.
But on the rich strip at night just driving
and looking around, listening to loud
music and not judging, not judging
even himself, he feels the TV
in his brain click off when the soft
white of a streetcar's headlamp—

blocks away—seems a false though lovely
offering for which words will not do,

and do not matter.

A RIDE

The young one is cheerful and kind.
The spread fingers of his hand are gentle
as they guide my head to miss the doorframe.
He tells how I may sit comfortably
with my sore knuckles behind me,
speaks calmly and frankly about my chances
of getting out by morning.
On the way to the station,
we converse through the silver vents
that line the Plexiglas shield.
The one who drives is distracted and weary;
at a stop he turns his wedding band,
stares over his shades at the three-tiered lights,
whistles three wretched bars of a dead melody.
The young one is younger than I,
inarticulate, eager, tethered firmly to the material world.
I think, in the midst of our chatter,
that there is no reason why he should not love his gun.
He asks what I do, and I tell him I write.
From that moment,
he speaks with excitement he tries to conceal.
In three or four minutes
he narrates several dangerous police adventures.
The driver is lost in thought.
I get the feeling the younger one
would like to know me better,
maybe be my friend.

He does not know, as the other does,
that I loathe him with my soul,
which does not exist
except at times like this.

Eating the Kennedys

It's ironic that famine brought them here,
for I'd shout, "President Kennedy!"
and my hunger shriveled.
I would not have to go to the corner store
and steal a Mars bar,
nor would I have to swipe pieces of food
from my sibling's hands.
We were often hungry
in a neighborhood of hunger,
a square half mile of boring angles of brick
at the farthest reaches of the New Frontier.
But a Kennedy was president,
swimming courageously over our heads,
and his whole huge family swam behind him,
the children dog-paddling or riding
their mother's backs,
and we, the entire nation,
rich and poor, black and white and other,
rose from the darkest depths
and ripped and tore at them,

or on Sundays, even after the slaughter in Dallas,
we'd make a ritual of it;
whole neighborhoods bellied up
to huge aluminum vats.

The joyous slurping and swilling
of millions eating great dripping
handfuls of Kennedy is a sound
for which I shall always feel nostalgia.

THESE ANGELS

These new angels are different, quite different.
One sees them gathered in packs of five or seven
in semicircles, bouncing on haunches,
phosphorescent in their nakedness,
pecking bits of flesh from road kill,
or playing a game with marked stones
similar to dice, but more complex.

They are the new idle rich,
or swell heaven's dole.
Either way, they don't pay taxes.

Therefore, I, nervous agnostic
vexed utterly by what I cannot know,
pray mechanically for their swift repatriation,
and write terse letters to my congresswoman.

LAFITTE

After one has been dead a long time,
The life he left gets conflated with others;
Then, drifting through changes, noting a few,
A soul may feel time as a body sweet
Fever coming on on a chilly night,
And so, if I did not live adventures
Of that rogue Lafitte, they adhere like the smell
Of dirty smoke to essential fabric
Of what I am and may presume to be.
When I stoop to haunt, I am Lafitte.

I blow above the corrugated tiles
And through the iron-black lacework of Vieux Carré,
Gleaning quaint passions of the living,
Those plush, adorable sensations they take
For ecstasy. Indeed, until one has died,
Until one has felt the light crack, then crumble
And spill forth the fury of negation,
Until one has been thereby anointed,
Warm secretions and mutual frictions
Are the pitiful measure of "transcendence."
Each death is a forever fuck, a passion
Beyond corporeal head or heart, without
Pretence of romance or "need" of anyone;
It is lived life, in all its particulars,
We the dead can't stop fucking, for to cease
Is to uncouple sentience from wonder,
And that's the fabled hell of gross self-knowledge.

I, Lafitte the blacksmith and storied rogue,
Therefore bear exquisite witness, and am charged
With ushering from their terror—through the lives
Of those who killed them—all the slaughtered ones
In this sector of the river's city.
That is, each victim may observe his own
Passing and know the shrill joy of his killer,
Feel the reciprocity of murder,
When that thief of his breath flees the dark market
Of his cooling flesh, to burn on the night
Like a television gnawing shadows.
And as I speak upon the nerves of this
Scribbler, this "poet," this wedge of pregnant cloth,
Even as he bellows forth, puffed with my
Fancy, rudderless but that I should rock
The swells, I, the dead pirate Jean Lafitte,
Am drawn to a crime as to a rich galleon.
The street shimmers in pale gaslight, and where
A pinched strip of Burgundy intersects
With Ursuline, an intermittent patch
Of jutting angles, shadows and flickerings,
Is occupied by one resolved to kill.
The footfall thickens, and the predator's heart
Blurs like gasping wings in an airless jar.
I pause to savor his adrenaline rush,
And even as the traffic on Rue Rampart
Seems a steady drizzle after midnight,
A battered cab glides through intersections,
Transmitting a clutch of drag queens to a joint
Up on Frenchman, and that boy, armed and filled

With a need and an anger, bangs his back
Against the radiating bricks, freezes,
Until the car is past and a quick glance
To all points confirms that no one is near,
No one but the mark, the pale idiot
Whose money might as well be boiling cabbage
It so stinks the air before him as he strides.
A savage blossoming of human wills
Records back, through separate bloodlines, until
Converging on the festered origin
Of tragic terror and necessity.
And all the trapped and useless dead applaud
Within the civic theater of nothing.
I give the victim his moment inside
The killer, the vision of his own demise,
And let him feel the rush of stripping his
Shocked self-becoming-corpse of gold watch, gold
Chain and tie clasp, thick wallet and shoes.
Then I let him drift among the stars awhile.
Then I let him find his place among the dead.

I, the rogue, blacksmith, pirate Jean Lafitte,
Or someone like him, or someone who loved
Someone like him, and was hurt unto death . . .

Perhaps I was a woman or a boy
Jilted by the cad, one who wore his shirt
To bed and wept until the sleeves were soggy.

Always, the torment of identity,
And the curious perspectives love affords . . .
There is no God, and He is merciful.

THE SURFER

Father, you needn't punish me anymore.
I shall punish myself now.

Sigmund Freud

Cold April ocean thrilled the surfer's skin
And shocked his brain alert; graphing the flow,
The first full minute after he sliced in,
Undulating upon the drift below
The shifting drifts of salty morning air,
He (serpentine) stared out at the charmed swells,
Forgot mere physics of how they could tear
White dripping roots that blurred to green then fell
To curling spread of aqua-smooth release.
That storied movement was destination.
Like one issued grim orders to police
A turbulent range defining nations,
Between the gray break-boulders at his lee
And a thin, sweeping sandbar, he shuttled
Parallel, as grieving to memory.
Sensation palpable as passion pulled
A part of him passion was not meant to reach,
The quiet, dry center where balance gripped
His spine, grapnelled his will onto the beach.
A buoy frigged upon the line where currents ripped
A quarter mile beyond where breakers rise.
He'd seen a tourist paddle out that far
To dumb-show for a lover, then heard the cries,

High rasps of terror diminished in air
Weighted with the ocean's contrabass.
Sex and dancing define repetition
In lyric terms of mirroring and pace.
This is what he does, what must be done,
When doing must be felt so he may feel.
Others waken to their dread and live it;
Dreading life, he wakens squatting in the peel
Of water pushing water to a limit
His mother voiced in pain when he was born.
His longest ride he always dreams his last.
Young men look back upon themselves and mourn
Futures in repetitions that are past.

V. From
Dithyrambs, 1998

Perhaps for all the wrong reasons, I am enchanted by the choral ejaculations of Attic tragedy, and am fascinated by the question of how tragic drama, the likes of which developed nowhere else on earth, issued from a particular moment in ancient history, the product of satyr plays, dithyrambs, and epics. As far as I can tell, what fragments of dithyrambs we have are not necessarily representative of those immediate precursors of Aeschylus's Oresteia, *and I imagine that one must look directly into Aeschylian drama to see the vestiges of dithyrambs in their latest development, a period when they were original compositions and not simply received, folkish forms.*

My dithyrambs are highly stylized blank-verse monologues framed by choral outbursts. In each of these poems, several dialectics are at play, not the least of which is a simultaneous yearning for, and parody of, a "high" lyric style.

The Child

Male and Female Chorus:
We shimmer through gilt surfaces of mist,
Or flit and buzz upon the stink of waste.
As clouds to granite peaks, or sex to death,
We are the essence of what faith conceals.

Male Chorus Leader:
Lucid to the end, my bright little one
Listened to the old stories, her hair fanned out
Over the pillow, her dark eyes intent
Upon the ceiling; I tried to say the words
With all the cheer her innocence required,
To make the fables serve as verbal bond
Between a father's need and daughter's wonder.
But as I mouthed the words and watched her face
Drain away that quick, sustained enchantment
Defining by its purity all hope,
Even before the light had left her eyes
I knew she was no more the child I'd loved.

Female Chorus:
Praise the lies that are our consolations.

Male Chorus Leader:
A quiet wisdom filled her tortured gaze,
As though inside that moment before death

Profundity was revealed that washed away
All innocence, and left her dull and sated.
I read on, several pages, to the end,
The happy ending of a fairytale
In which the princess blah blah blah blah blah,
After I knew my little girl was gone.

MALE CHORUS:
Praise the cold lights of cities far away.
Praise stars that are the daughters of all darkness.

FEMALE CHORUS LEADER:
There is nothing left between us, yet still
We scavenge the ruins of the other.
I take his hand in the night, and squeeze, as though
Small intimacies still were possible.
No joy, not even old sardonic humor
Of memories saved against such pain as this
Suffices, for as our present bleeds into
A future of intolerable loss,
So our past is now intolerable.
We mumble over meals of starting over,
Of other children who may compensate.
But we know there is no compensation.
We are lost within the details of our loss,
And live not together, but juxtaposed.

FEMALE CHORUS:
Praise all our burdens larger than the sky.

134

Praise delicate shavings of our wooden hearts.
Praise deaf, mute angels who graze among the beasts.

FEMALE CHORUS LEADER:
I was contented with their special closeness,
Which didn't exclude so much as ignore.
I knew she might flit between us for years,
Favoring one and then the other, until
She danced away, and we became one thing,
Her single point from which to keep a distance.
As she grew ill, she called for him in the day,
But after dark for me. I was her sleep,
Her sole diversion from the swelling terror.

MALE CHORUS LEADER:
The world we made was sweeter than the world,
More just, of course, but also filled with dangers,
Quite insurmountable it seemed, except
For our *deus ex machina*, her magic.
When trolls or giants threatened her, a wave
Of wand or other charming trinket pressed
Into the service of her will saved worlds.
Such powers as hers a father might envy, but
That his child, his truest love, possessed it.

FEMALE CHORUS:
If suddenly you wake, alone and scared
To be alone, consider coldly the hour
Of your passing, the hurt breathing, prolonged

By the body's will, other than your own,
Or that it happens violently, the glass
Splashing all around the buckling steel,
And concussion like a drum: you are the drum.

MALE CHORUS:
Praise neon flash against the pitch of night.
Praise laughter stumbling through an unlit morning.
Praise boys in bodies of strong men cursing
The first fay light, then falling to their knees.

FEMALE CHORUS LEADER:
I stare at him across a room. He reads.
He wets his finger, flips the page. The sun-
Light edging through the curtain streaks and blanches
One ruddy cheek and baggy eye. He blinks
And squints a bit against the light, the light
Which in a moment softens, slips away.
He shifts his glasses, glances at the clock,
Rises painfully, pads into the den.
The clink, the click, the popping of the cubes,
The long fall into fitful sleep in which
He often thrashes, weeps, and moans her name.

MALE AND FEMALE CHORUS:
Consider stepping slowly into flames
As though to do so were a luxury.

FEMALE CHORUS:
Praise the waxed corridors of public buildings.
Praise the frowns and furrowed brows of specialists.
Praise hothouse flowers in almost every window.

MALE CHORUS:
Praise those who suffer unabashedly.

FEMALE CHORUS:
Praise those who curl up in the dark and weep.

MALE CHORUS:
Praise those who weep as though to weep forever.

FEMALE CHORUS:
Praise suicide in verdant, quiet places.

MALE CHORUS:
Praise all who suffer life to live, and live.

MALE CHORUS LEADER:
I have held the tart barrel on my tongue,
A sentimental gesture, yes, and quite
Irrelevant, or, at least, self-mocking.
The pain of loss is all I have of her.
To lose myself would be to lose even that.
And this is not a coward's consolation.
When the pain is exhausted, frazzled, numb,
I'll take the quick ride on eternity.

FEMALE CHORUS LEADER:
I've grown concerned beyond my own shrill pain.
I trace the contours of his thoughts against
His will, and know they burn, shriek, and dovetail
With a single image, then arc upon
A flash of longing into oblivion.

FEMALE AND MALE CHORUS:
Inscribed upon the brutish heart of each
Self-marveling, fooling man are litanies
Of crimes he would contrive if world were blind.
The wish to fill a universe completely,
Supplant all matter, subsume all light, until
There is only the one masculine will
Throbbing within, upon, about itself,
Determines heft and depth of lyric sorrow.
For where but in the fixed command to breed
Resides the hell and bliss of what we are?
Those who rescue beauty, love, and pride
From the reeking pit of procreation
Will simulate the dateless birth of God,
And know too late the pit itself divine.

FEMALE CHORUS:
What lies are these we tally in our dreams?

MALE CHORUS:
What dreams are these in which we stow our sins?

FEMALE CHORUS:
May victims plead no more with evil men.
May false dawns kiss no more the fields of death.
May cries recede to the hushed banks of sleep.

MALE CHORUS:
Praise the great river from which all sorrow flows.

FEMALE CHORUS:
Praise redundant rains that swell the river.

FEMALE CHORUS LEADER:
Praise reciprocity of rains and rivers.

FEMALE CHORUS LEADER:
Our marriage was not born of romance, but then
Our lives were bound by stronger promises
Than tether those ephemeral affections
Wilder hearts will rue when passions cool.
We grew into a comfort that soon slipped
Into a numbness not at all unpleasant.
He seemed to need so little of me, and I
Required his acquiescent presence only.
A decade passed. A piece of another turned
It seemed to mist and blew away. The grave,
I guess, seemed not imminent, but closer, close
Enough, quite suddenly, it seemed, for him,
I say it seemed for him, but not for me,
That we should open out our lives and try
To make a life to haunt when we are gone.

FEMALE CHORUS:
Praise news of death we read in children's eyes.

MALE CHORUS LEADER:
I did not resent her need for comfort,
And respected always the sacrifice
She made to drop the child into our lives.
It was a gift, I knew, from her to me,
Beyond implicit contracts we had forged,
A friendship token I was grateful for,
And promised solemnly to bear the weight
Of nasty little daily infamies.
But through the pregnancy she changed.
The act begun abstractly as accretion,
A waiting for a process too complex
To understand except in broadest terms,
Became a mystery she took to heart.

MALE CHORUS:
Praise all changes of the protean heart.

MALE CHORUS LEADER:
And so the child was hers through birth and after,
And I was household helper, hired hand
To fetch and tote and clean up after them.
And I was happy, happy in the role,
And marveled at the bond, the natural bond
Between a woman's and an infant's needs.
To my consciousness, they became an it,

A single thing outside of us yet still
Within such intimate proximity
We danced in fixed and elegant orbit of
The same cosmic consequences, the same
Vague, magnificent, fate-filled potency.

FEMALE CHORUS:
May love become a grave contingency.

MALE CHORUS:
Praise miles of dirt packed thick with bulbs and seeds.

FEMALE CHORUS:
May myths of love not blur the thing itself.

MALE CHORUS:
Praise the harvest! Praise abundance! Praise life!

FEMALE CHORUS LEADER:
It was in language he made his bond with her.
In myths and legends, explanations of
The pictures in the books he read aloud
Each night, his voice became the voice of time,
And voice of naming things, and how they work,
And why, and why and why and why and why.
When she was barely old enough to talk,
When she could barely talk they talked for hours.
His interest never flagged; he sat and calmly
Listened, then calmly answered every question,

Or simply nodded affirmation as
She babbled on from point to childish point.
He repossessed his world, through words, through her.
And as she grew into the language, past
Babble into a reasoned, smart regard
Of fabula and what she daily witnessed,
So his world deepened such that what had been
Vexations, horrors, threats, affronts and schemes
Became in sum the mystery of life,
That which he would prepare her for before
He passed from mystery to mystery.

FEMALE AND MALE CHORUS:
Praise heart's surrender to the small and mild.

FEMALE CHORUS LEADER:
His silence now is haunted by her voice.
He listens to each word she doesn't say.
My heart may not surrender to her loss
As long as I must mourn his mourning her.
I walk out to the garden, touch each rose,
Pick away a few dead leaves, caress a thorn.
Magnolias nod their gaudy blooms like old
Bewitching mothers soon to curl, and die.
They are so much clumsier than the roses.
Yet I love them more than any flower.
I love the rich creaminess of their of their petals.
I love how comical they are in death,
Their rotting skins hugging to the compost

Like happy drunkards singing to themselves.
My baby's gone, and legions of roses spill
Their sexual softness after her upon
The huge and perfect lap that death becomes.

THE DIVORCE

FEMALE CHORUS:
Where there are solar systems with two stars,
Surely fate of one determines other;
But though one flares much brighter than its mate,
Or spins for eons swifter on its pole,
When one must surge, collapse, then throb, then fade,
May other burn alone as though alone?
If one implodes into a pit of darkness,
The two are no less coupled than before.
Once coupled, no matter changes that occur
To one or both, two fates are single fate.

MALE CHORUS:
Praise desire to become a thing apart.

FEMALE CHORUS LEADER:
Of course it shatters confidence of all
Who'd cared for them as something singular.
One couldn't utter name of one and not
Also speak of other, as though each were
But residue of other, such that each,
Autonomous, distinct, existed yet
To complement the other's graceful life.
So confidence in one's own mating bond
At least is shaken in such times as these
When two, who seemed to cleave so naturally,
Without forebodings suddenly must turn
Away from expectations and each other.

MALE CHORUS:
Praise those who lie alone in beds of grief
Because they rose from beds to tell the truth.

MALE CHORUS LEADER:
I think she's touched more deeply by the split
Than I, if only for the fact that she
Had known them longer as a doting pair.
I never really liked him much, perhaps
Because I've never meshed with men who seem
To cultivate their sensitivity
And make a subtle show of tenderness.
I frankly knew that they were doomed when once
I saw him being sensitive with a sad
And gorgeous woman who had sought him out;
Indeed, I have no doubt she sought his help.
They occupied a booth behind a window,
And kept their hands around their coffee cups.
I paused out on the street and just observed
How he tilted his head attentively
And wrinkled up his brow, and frowned, and shook
His head as if in utter disbelief
That any man could hurt a joy like her.
And then, of course, he touched her hand, and then,
Of course, he touched her cheek, and I pushed on.
Perhaps he is authentically that way.
Perhaps, indeed, no hidden agenda lurked

Behind his show of sweetness to that woman.
Perhaps I simply cast my own dark thoughts,
My own lascivious desires unto him.
Perhaps a man can be what he appears.
However, I find him difficult to take
But never must appear to find him so.
Oh, God, I'd love to know he left his wife
For younger stuff, or, better yet, a man!

FEMALE CHORUS:
Praise her who walks away with dignity.

MALE CHORUS:
Praise him who walks away with dignity.

FEMALE CHORUS AND MALE CHORUS:
False dignity is born of feigned affection.

FEMALE CHORUS LEADER:
He seems quite fond of both, yet not surprised
When told by mutual friends the marriage died.
I was devastated, shocked silent by
The news, in retrospect more deeply moved
Than such events, in such a world as ours,
Should reasonably affect in one who's watched
A dozen marriages dissolve as through
A microscope one watches mold advance.
As news of their demise—for "they" are dead—
Washed over me, I stared across the table

To where he slouched, the candle flicking him,
His crock of bisque steaming in his face.
I wanted him to glance at me, to say
With tender look or grin that we're all right,
That our one life is indivisible.
But he was curious for news of details,
And pressed our friends to talk out all the dirt.
Was one, or both, involved with someone else?
Was he a cheating bastard in sheep's clothing?
Did she or he initiate the break?
I knew our marriage bond was unto death.
I knew that though he lived distracted, hunched
Within himself, he must have me for light,
For those occasions when he crawls outside
Himself and, squinting, sniffs the air and stretches,
Then roams about through stiff congenial gossip.
He must have me to charm the world he loathes
But cannot manage to avoid, and I
Can play the part of cheery antidote
To his dyspeptic gloom so well that some
Are simply moved by starkness of the contrast.
We've been a hit for years among our friends,
Or, rather, the friendships I sustain in spite
Of him, the friendships that he tolerates.

MALE CHORUS:
Praise gray sustaining solitary moods
In midst of those few others who reveal,
With subtle gestures, subtle ruthlessness.

Praise impulse to recede within a state
Of insincere congeniality.

MALE CHORUS LEADER:
I actually found her mildly interesting,
Quite attractive, and once enjoyed a talk
We had at some pretentious dinner party
Where he held forth, tastefully of course, about
A poor endangered species in a place
Whose name seemed not to have a vowel, and where
The local custom was to eat the thing
Exclusively each day of rainy season.
We spoke of recipes for dog she'd read
Translated from Chinese, and laughed out loud
When fluffy yappers of our host went off
At small disturbances in neighbors' yards.
So then I sensed the fissure in their lives,
Their temperaments, the ways they viewed the world.

FEMALE CHORUS:
Behold the silent signal of distress.

MALE CHORUS LEADER:
And wondered if she found appealing such
A man as I who views sardonically
The vast corrosive world of otherness,
For surely living in the shadow of
A saint, as I do too, for her must be
As stifling as a cloister on a hill,

A place whose verve pale piety has sapped.
Similar to me, she seems addicted
To his goodness, to how the world is drawn
To him and calmed by all he thinks and says,
As though it seems to others that if one
So dedicated to a decent life
Of utterly engaged transparency
Can live among them, surely their own sins
Of quaint duplicity might be diminished.
I glanced across the room at my own mate,
My graceful, quiet, good, and decent wife,
And caught her earnestly engaged in talk
With my poor interlocutor's good man.
Their brows seemed stitched with furrowed flags of deep
Concern for whales and starving children, soil
Erosion, baby seals, and global warming,
And so it seemed their heads prepared to sail
Heroically away upon their vast
Tumultuous ocean of regard for others.
And there we stood, addicted to their goodness,
Ironical, conflicted, paralyzed,
Just watching, always watching from the shore.

FEMALE CHORUS LEADER:
He's always been there for me, or for himself,
Perhaps, though for my sake at least in terms
Of ignorant effect, for I've assumed
Him faithful keeper of my secret life,
The taciturn yet noble lover of

The truth of what I am and seek to be,
And I until the troubling breach have stood
Transparent in my every word to him.
Yet now I peer into the man I've loved
And cannot see beyond his surface; it seems
That tiny mirrors hang all over him,
And black oil pools the spaces in between.
There is no revelation in this life
As when the most familiar thing one knows
Becomes with stunning suddenness more foreign
Than quantum weirdness to an average mind.
I wonder if it was that way with her,
Though likelier I think that she transformed
To his more trusting eyes, becoming one
Not cruel, unfaithful, tactless or malign,
But shattered at the core such that to lift
Her like a doll and shake would be to hear
A thousand tiny shards rattling like rice,
Or filaments of plastic trapped within.
And yet it seems now that the world divides
This way, between the solid and the shattered,
Between the guileless lover and beguiled
Beloved, and usually one will find
The other, though happiness is possible
For either only with its own kind near:
A shattered core should find a shattered core,
And solid one to solid one is bliss.
Lover to lover, beloved to itself...

MALE CHORUS LEADER:

One time, when we were young, I held her tight
In the middle of a crowd. New Years, I think,
Or Independence Day; I can't recall
If we were dressed for chill or summer warmth,
Nor even can I conjure if we stood
Upon a city square or golf course green
Beneath the booming blooms of fireworks.
I only know that moment I was moved
By her proximity to glimpse my death,
And at that moment we were bound together.
The question, the question that defines my life
Is whether our untethering would be
A glimpse of life, of what is possible
In time so brief, or whether it would seem
A diminution I would suffer yet
Unto myself, unto eternity.

FEMALE CHORUS LEADER:

Divorce by definition is to turn
Away, and so by etymology
We are, perhaps, divorced, and have been for
So many years I'm frightened to recall
If there was a moment it occurred,
A fixed point in our lives I might remember.
I do recall the moment he was mine.
We'd strolled out to the pier one autumn night
When city fathers had decided to
Display our civic pride back to ourselves.

It was the anniversary of when
Some klutz in eighteen eighty-something signed
The charter that our hometown issued from,
And pyrotechnics lit the sky, as one
Young man held one young woman and shivered there
Beneath the stars and blue and golden blooms,
Amid the slack-jawed neighbors of their youth.
I saw then in his eyes that I was his,
And realize now our lives are mortgaged to
Our first enchantment, and that we've finally paid
The last installment, and only now may say
We own outright the life each lost to it.

FEMALE CHORUS:
Praise solitary life in middle years.

MALE CHORUS:
Beware unclasping lives in middle years.

FEMALE AND MALE CHORUS:
There is never freedom from the other.
The other is a presence unto death.
˩ ˙s the gesture of rejection where
sides the radical new life one seeks,
ᴅd it is fleeting yet sustaining as
ᴇnew fixed point from which to leave the world.

ˉALE CHORUS LEADER:
n paralyzed to act upon desire.

FEMALE CHORUS LEADER:
Released unto myself, I'll walk away,
And though I'll drag his essence after me,
I'll make of it a thing to stash inside
A box and place up high upon a shelf.

BROTHER LOVE

CHORUS (MALE AND FEMALE)
The fibrillations of man's sorrow,
Brief consequence of terror in self-knowledge,
Presage a bottomless plunge towards solitude.
Perhaps he cries for all the pain he's caused.
Perhaps he curls up in the dark and sobs.
Perhaps he presses death between his eyes
And squeezes off his one unselfish act.
But each lucky man has one brother in pain,
His life lived otherwise, or parallel.

GAY BROTHER:
I have done one terrible thing. I was born.
I have performed one great act many times.

STRAIGHT BROTHER:
To think the same woman gave breath to us,
The same man coaxed us from the permutations
Of his marvelous body's difficult code.

GAY BROTHER:
In those woods behind our uncle's house
A path as narrow as a boy's quick stride
Burned serpentine through brush to the black stream.

CHORUS:
Praise innocent journeys on summer days.

154

GAY BROTHER:
By the fallen enormous trunk of oak
That breached the breadth of the small water's flow,
I found a dirty piece of cloth, some boy's
Shed briefs he'd tossed aside before plunging in.

CHORUS:
Praise sweet guilt of confused awakenings.

STRAIGHT BROTHER:
I think I knew his body's revelation.
I think I knew the day he found his path.

GAY BROTHER:
I plucked it up, and brushed it off, and held
It to my cheek, and felt a sobbing rage
Rush through my groin, and realized friendship meant
To me a thing, an act, a symmetry
That other boys would fear and wish to kill.

STRAIGHT BROTHER:
Fraternal twins, our raw coterminous fates
Distinct at birth but mutually determined,
We grew into an intimate self-loathing
Indicative of primal brother love.

CHORUS:

At inception, God the baby wept and wailed
To conjure forth a flash and silver surface,
And seeing that It was a lovely God,
Cooed Itself a sphere of machinations,
Of whirling contradictions signifying
Each to each the essence of necessity.

STRAIGHT BROTHER:

We lay in separate beds and whispered dreams
And lies and boasted, as our father did,
That we would have the world for ransoming.
He was my passionate foe and confidant.
When we touched, it was for brutal pleasure,
Wrestling on the fragrant morning grass.

CHORUS:

Praise the angular beauty of the day.
Praise the frank inconstant stars and summer skies.
Praise the stiffening contours of the night.

STRAIGHT BROTHER:

But then it seemed a sentimental pall
Of adolescent doom covered him in smoke,
And he stepped forth another than I had known.
He read of chivalric lives—always soft,
Fair, and verdant—idyllic nobility,
As though on the plane of fiction and dreams,
Where nothing shits nor flies insult the air,

His rooting, squealing new desire might sleep.
I did not have the heart for what he was,
And just the faintest concept of the laws
Of nature his abomination cursed.
Several humid nights I followed him to town
And observed him lounging on a gas-lit stoop
Until a fatherly car would slow, open,
And brother of my flesh would pause, then enter.
Shocked, unfamiliar with the symptoms of grief,
I strangled soft affection for his name.

CHORUS:
He who awakens to his mortal difference,
He who is changed and suffers change, will plunge
Into Death's tangled currents and emerge
Gasping, dripping mortality, coughing prayers.

GAY BROTHER:
First I was darling of the dirty secrets,
The cloistered fancy of the timid butch.
"Just think of my as your special daddy,"
one pink-skinned balding Volvo told me.
Later, I found a crayon on the seat
In back, and slipped it in my pocket with
The bills he slipped me before he sped away.
But I wanted love, not old men's money.
I wanted a special friend, like a brother,
Only more intimate, rough yet tender.

CHORUS:

The burning issues on the tongues of angels
Are heaven's forfeitures of reasoned mercy.
When God pontificates, the speed of light
Is that at which the throngs of blessed ones pass
From bliss to boredom, to nodding somnolence.

GAY BROTHER:

Romantic, pale, hazed light of surrender,
The whole round thing stopped the night like a cork.
A starry effervescence seemed to hiss
With joy I heard but could not see, face-down
As I was in grass, my lover's fingers wound
Through my hair as though I galloped in the dark.

STRAIGHT BROTHER:

I gazed over the rim of a stinking can,
Not twenty yards from where a writhing flower
Shed violent silhouettes across the brink
Of shrubs and stones that lined the river bank.
What churning pain was this that he called love?
What rank humiliations drove his needs?
Persecution halted with terminal grunts.
The agent of pain backed out like a cat,
Drew up the denim gathered at his ankles,
Sniffed and smirked at the indolent moon, then strolled
Towards spangled city streets, smoothing his hair.
My brother lifted to his elbows, then knees,
His face pouring down like a snapped blossom.

CHORUS:

Deep zones of mystery are passing away.
Great healing jungles are aching with flames.
The waters are choking. Skies dissipate.
Who, seeking love, should wish procreation?

STRAIGHT BROTHER:

He beat me for the sake of filial love,
A father's proud desire that sons should be
The living monuments of how he lived.
There was of course a ritual to it all.
Feeling left his face like draining liquid,
And he stood as still as God the longest moment,
Until he slowly pointed to the hook
Where his razor strap would droop like bacon.
The offender's part was to fetch it to him
Then lay across the couch arm, mute supplicant,
Pants down. But he would sometimes make us wait.
Often a sweaty minute, one time with me
An hour before he lashed my flesh five times
Ferociously. The pain would burn for days.
But once, I don't know why, my brother lay
Bare-assed across the couch arm for an hour,
Then another, until the house grew dark
And still he did not move or father come
To lash him for some boyish indiscretion.
That morning I awakened to his weeping,
And when I peered across the banister
I saw him still arched over, fouled and wet,
Sobbing for forgiveness, begging for pain.

CHORUS:

When angels mourn, the lamps grow dim in nurseries,
And newborns paw the air and cast blurred eyes
Upon dark ceilings, where the new dead float.
The infants, whose brief souls are angel's tears,
Are so pristine the blessed can but weep the more,
Though new dead grumble for a quick revenge
On those who weep to weep that perfect soul
Whose nature is the slide to such corruption
As they, being dead, escaped yet yearn for still.

GAY BROTHER:

That world I found within the world was true
To those shrill longings chanting in my blood.
When acrimony of my father's voice
Intensified beyond what I could bear,
When the world outside my world had choked with shame
For what by nature, or unnatural design—
The difference to my heart is only words—
My body's separate will had shunned convention,
I orphaned my soul, speculation's breath,
Unto the living city's lap of danger,
Where no mother's sighs, father's rage, brother's shock
Could burst exquisite dreams of satisfaction.

CHORUS:

Praise the blank wall where many families weep
A sorrow greater than the world's blue turning.
Praise the falling fist and flinching brow.

STRAIGHT BROTHER:

These twenty years since I twice saw him so,
Deranged and glowing with humiliation,
My righteousness has softened for the wisdom
That I have since curled over for a few
No less inglorious humiliations,
And if he remains a mortal mystery to
Me still, I am puzzled with affection.
He lay now, rasping breaths, punk to a system
More concerned with bed space than with healing.
Is there a less ennobling sphere of passage
Than this dull chrome and linen house of numbness?
White smocks pass through; like me they only wait.
I do not blame them for their helplessness,
Though their officious posturing revolts.
Gloved, the attendants turn him gingerly
And adjust the hissing nozzle in his mouth.
Ashen, diminished-to-bone, unconscious thing,
He seems a hatchling fallen from its nest.
I would cup it in my hands and, running
To the house, shout, "Mother! Look what I have found!"

CHORUS:

Praise brief horror that is the death of dying.

STRAIGHT BROTHER:

But she would not be there, or anyone else,
Only he as a small boy, reading his book.
He would stare into my hands, then look up

And smile a worried smile into my eyes.
Together we would fashion a cotton nest
And keep it, a day or two, between our beds.

VI. FROM
PRAGUE WINTER, 2004

Rehab

Two springs, I filled our rooms with chirping fleets
of fledglings quiet women of the zoo's
Bird Rehab Center fetched from fallen nests.
My tasks were just to feed them, keep them warm
and shoo away the cats that gathered on
the balcony above our lush courtyard.
Mockers, jays, tough proletarian birds
grew fast and pulsed away; though even as
I brought more tiny eaters home in boxes,
the grown ones gathered every morning, into
summer, on the railing of the balcony
at 6:15 a.m., and squawked until
I stumbled out and dropped a pinch of moist
cat food down each screamer's gullet, to bid
it pop upon the air and disappear.
Then I padded in and fed the babies.

Those were good years in a marriage most would judge
a good one, all in all. We worked hard and laughed
a lot, pursuing separate interests, and came
together every night with no agenda
but the comfort of our coupling, and sleep.

When the weak ones shriveled, I grew despondent,
isolating them until they died or
rallied, and when they quit their begging, and when
their hideous small faces—the bulging

monster eyes lidded with veins—dangled back
upon their too-delicate necks, I cupped
them in one hand and stroked them with a finger
until the last perceptible breaths had ceased.

THE DOG

As my colleague drives me to work, a brown dog
lopes into the street. A subdued lover of
lost creatures, a woman who lives alone
but for her two infirm beloved mutts,
she swerves and touches her breasts, relieved to be
beyond the event horizon of that doom.
She doesn't look back, and neither, in fact, shall I.
Surely the dazed thing was kept for years and then
rejected, or simply drawn by odors
down long blocks of odors toward the moment,
lost and drunk on all that olfactory wisdom,
he careened onto the blacktop and through
the lives of several lucky drivers, and one
life fated for a morning's inconvenience

On the pleasant span between the bayou
and the golf course, our conversation veers
from whether unused sick-leave time might count
toward that sixty-percent-of-base-pay bliss
We've both begun to dream of, and whether next
year our Agenda for a Better Way
will win the hearts and minds of wary colleagues,
and lights awhile upon my sweet ex-wife.
Otherwise vicious in our gossiping,
we are tender, always tender when we speak
of her, of her travails and conquests since
the marriage—always it is "the marriage"—

died such that all "we" were became a thing
outside of "us," and wanders still the gross
contingencies, the foul and bitter ground
of where it seemed, together, we would go.

The Car, the House

If I were rich, and my blood blue, I'd lay
Before your feet dear things and stacks of cash.
My imperial guilt would swell and groan to hand
You all that might sustain a delicate life.
Though you are not delicate, only wronged.
A childless marriage is a luxury,
Neither necessary nor advisable,
Until age or some great illness lays one out.
Yet tethered so, the coupled heart may tug
Against its bond, but if it pulls away . . .
This is just to say, dear, I was a prick,
And an asshole, and every other foul,
Despicable thing a woman wronged may scream.
As you nickel and dime me, darling, for
A monthly stipend none would say I owe
Except perhaps your mother and your lawyer;
As you, sweetheart, unburden me of just
Enough to make me wince each month to scrawl
My signature beneath our family name,
To which the pinched sum is made payable;
I'm healed, a little, as if by leeches,
And so it seems some ancient cures still hold
Their uses, though ancient punishments should be
The choice of one like you, so wronged so long.
Let every woman hurt pick up a stone
Against the man who lay down with another!
Let all her friends and family, and even some

Of his, ring the deep pit to help her pelt him!
Good woman, beautiful best friend of my youth,
The car, the house are yours; the debts are mine.

SAINT ROCH

We rented in the Quarter several years,
Then bought a modest two-floor wooden house
Ten blocks—and worlds—away, on a Ninth Ward street
Named for a saint assigned to hear bleak cases,
A goofy street as gay as straight, black as white,
As working-class as new-rich gentrified.
It was a perfect place not to raise a child,
To be an arty couple, youthful but
Not young enough to feel that we were young.
And I was superficially happy there,
And must assume she was genuinely so,
For when our marriage fell apart, that is,
When I dismantled it so clumsily,
She seemed a part of her was in a coma.

From the window above the stairs, one could
Not help but gaze into the trashy yard
That butted up against our property,
Especially when the cackling began.
Almost every day that boy would howl,
Rocking violently at the center of
The yard, in the midst of broken pipes, broken
Pieces of appliances, and gray planks
Strewn over scattered piles of busted bricks.
I call him a boy, but he was over
Thirty, and, standing in the rubble,
Rocked until it seemed he'd fly

Apart. But revved up to his limit, he'd keep
His furious pace for hours, worse than any
Bad neighbor's bad dog, and yet we rather
Liked him, or the idea of him, and did
Not lodge complaint. Yet as the marriage sank
To hell, I couldn't hear his voice and watch
Him rocking in a joyful fury and
Not feel his ecstasy a mockery.
Almost every day the idiot achieved
A bliss, it seemed, independent of his life,
For how could such a creature know such joy
From rank particulars of such a life?
How could he be so wise and yet so vacant?
So wretched in particulars yet blessed?

Last week, I walked my daughters through the church
In Vysehrad, in Prague. The four-year-old
Was not impressed, but being full of lunch
Was quiet in her mild distraction; the ten-
Year-old chattered rapid-fire inquiries.
Of the numerous gilded figures on the walls
And columns, several saints stared calmly out:
What is a saint? my oldest daughter asked.
It is a person who survives great pain
And, preserving faith, does impossible things.
Faith in what? What kinds of impossible things?
I answered as best I could, without faith,
And she seemed satisfied, but then she asked
About each saint, needing details, and I

Was stumped by most, but said Saint Roch was charged
By heaven with listening to the sickest lives,
And as I droned on, again holding forth
To one who is the juicy core of joy
About a subject I know nothing of
But ill-remembered facts, I thought of how
A saint of poorest health may spend his time
Alone, in heaven, amid the rubble there.

SECOND MARRIAGE

I am embarrassed by all my old poems,
as a wise poet said I would someday be.
"Someday" arrived in increments, broken
promises to a dear friend who thought me
wholly incapable of deception,
though in fact lying to her was easy,
even, in some grotesque way, necessary.

When I hold my daughters, the fruits of my
deception; when I tickle them till they
shriek and punch me again and again,
shrieking; when my girls are so
happy they scream and punch me and climb
on me shrieking for more, more tickles, more hugs,
more wrestling on the bed before they sleep;
when my daughters are so alive to all
I am and all they are, the lie of life,
that is, the lie that life is telling for
the moment, is our uncluttered joy,
and though it justifies nothing I have done,
there is nothing sullied it does not cleanse.

LOVE POEM FOR AN ENEMY

I, as sinned against as sinning,
Take small pleasure from the winning
Of our decades-long guerrilla war.
For from my job I've wanted more
Than victory over one who'd tried
To punish me before he died,
And now, neither of us dead,
We haunt these halls in constant dread
Of drifting past the other's life
While long-term memory is rife
With slights that sting like paper cuts.
We've occupied our separate ruts
Yet simmered in a single rage.
We've grown absurd in middle age
Together, and should seek wisdom now
Together, by finishing this row.
I therefore decommission you
As constant flagship of my rue.
Below the threshold of my hate
You now my good regard may rate.
For I have let my anger pass.
But, while you're down there, kiss my ass.

THE BOXERS EMBRACE

In Prague or in New Orleans, my perfect night
Of guilty pleasure is to watch a fight.

I know that it is heartless past all speech
To thrill at two men's pain as both must reach

Across the bloody billion-year abyss
To strike the other one, or make him miss.

Yet when I gaze upon the frank despair
Of spirit-broken people who must bear

The torments of cool fiends they cannot see—
Systemic meanness and brutality

Of bureaucratic processes that hide
The facts of who has profited and lied—

I see inside the grotesque and plodding dance
Of boxers something beautiful: a chance

To mediate the passions of the tribe
By what the ritual of fights describe

(As arm a sudden arc upon the gleam
within that space); for public fights redeem

Our sense of being, at once, in and out
Of nature, and so map the human route

Across the razor's edge of slow extinction,
Such is the truth of all destructive action,

Transcending histories of consequence
And serving therefore as a mottled lens

Unto the bifurcated human heart
Whose one true nature is to break apart

Revealing beast and angel wrapping arms
Beyond all consequence of temporal harms.

As systems fade, transform, reconstitute,
The fools will blather and the wise stand mute,

Then innocence must suffer out of reach
And over time our best intentions leach

Through all the lies we hold as history.
No yearning human heart is ever free,

Except when it has found its one true base,
Where the last bell rings, and the boxers embrace.

On the Day after Allen Ginsberg's Death
Someone Thinks of Me

for Gail Wronsky

A woman phones whom I've not seen
In eighteen years and didn't know
That well. She seems put off a bit
When I don't recognize her name,
But speaks of Charlottesville and folks
We knew in common, for an awkward
Minute, until my memory
Unclogs and spills forth images.
She called, she says, just to tell me
She remembers a party where
I punched some guy who, drunk and full
Of lip-curled swagger, had loudly cursed
My quoting Ginsberg's poems of love
To an arc of puzzled co-eds.
Of course, I didn't just turn around
And clock him. I tried to reason first,
Persuade him to my point of view
That Ginsberg wrote great poems and pounds
Of fluff, but that the fluff cannot
Muffle all the sweetness, or all
The charged and crazy posturing
And fresh iconoclastic yelping
And magnificent confounding of
The public and the private realms,

And then I whacked him. Of course I was
A fool, and that dyspeptic guy
Did not deserve a fool's reproach.
I'd forgotten all about that night
Until the woman phoned to mark
From half a continent away
That she recalls a night I fought,
On the porch of a house I would
Not recognize these days, about
A man who set his life against
Such childishness and schoolboy pride.
It was an ugly little fight
That others wisely stopped before
We really hurt our drunken selves,
And which of us was judged, by all
Who'd witnessed our brief dance, the bigger
Ass I cannot know and don't much care.
The fool I am forgives the fool
I was, and hopes the guy I punched
Can say the same. Though both of us
May feel small consolation in
The fact that our grotesque display
Is now odd theater in the mind
Of one recalling how a man,
In art, had married art and life
As no one ever will again.

PARIAH

Until you piss off an entire community, you may know nothing of bliss. For bliss, as I conceive it here, is freedom from the obligations of tact.

Colleague A nods as he passes. "You haven't published in decades," I say with a smile, nodding back. Colleague B gives a little wave with her free hand as she reaches for her mail. "Still sleeping with the dean?" I ask, rubbing the air between us with my palm. Our secretary, who knows better by now than to lift her eyes from the nonsense on her desk when I pass, just stiffens. Our chairman, though, cannot help himself. He rushes into the hall when the taps on my shoes clatter past his office. "You are evil!" he shouts. We all hate you!"

To which I do not reply, because I am headed for the Faculty Lounge where I must post fake snapshots, on the corkboard above the microwave, of his wife engaging our new medievalist, naked.

George W. Bush Was Very Nice to Me

as Bacchus rolled down St. Charles, and I chatted with him about politics, local and national, especially the eleven-fingered idiot running against David Duke for the Republican nomination for Fuhrer of the Suburbs. I told him flat out I hate the Republican Party and still he was nice to me, stood next to me, in the back of the ten-deep crowd that yelled for trinkets, and chatted for several minutes as though he really liked me, and didn't mind at all that I'd ripped a fine white string of beads from his grasp when he'd grabbed it from the air at the same time as I. As we chatted about Duke and New Orleans apartheid, about my having recently lived in the French Quarter and about how the trees on St. Charles seem for months after Carnival—indeed on some stretches all year round—like bearers of many-colored fruit from where the bead strands get caught in the branches, I knew I would one day write about meeting a president's goofy son, a nice guy, which is to say someone you shouldn't mind standing around shooting the breeze with on a pleasant spring night in New Orleans, though not someone you'd want to be cooped up with on a long drive, say, from El Paso to San Antonio, or certainly not from one paradigm to another.

The Letters

She's shouting at my face that her room
is wretchedly inadequate in terms
of size and window-space and furnishing
and that I'm responsible for this
tragedy and she'll have my head, or worse,
if at this very second I will fail
to move her to another room with big
bright windows, a softer bed, and of course
she will not share her space with anyone.

I know she has not slept in thirty hours,
and just the bus ride from the airport is
enough to trigger culture shock, and though
I want to shake her like a dog a sock
I smile and promise I will move her to
another room, then drag her baggage down
the hall, obsequious, burning to please.

She has arrived from the United States,
in Prague to study writing for a month,
and she already wishes she'd not come.
In her fifties, fairly well off, or spoiled
by plenty from my point of view as one
who must insure she gets her money's worth,
she is that kind of American harpy
who terrorizes waiters, salesmen, all
working stiffs who shoulder the wheel of commerce.

And when, just minutes after she has moved
to what's, by standards of this dorm, a penthouse,
I see her trotting, literally, up the hall
again towards me, I swallow, groan, and wince
then brace for dead bugs on the windowsill,
used condoms hanging from the shower rod,
or rats fucking loudly in the closet,
but she is waving pages in the air
and, halting, breathless, wild-eyed, sputters that
she needs translations of these letters, do
I know of anyone who at this hour
will translate them, for she has come to Prague
to see where her family lived before the war,
where uncles, aunts, and cousins made their homes,
where her mother's father owned great buildings
he himself designed, and where now no one
of her blood remains, no one, and only these
old letters, yellowed, brittle, in a tongue
she recalls the music of but cannot speak,
remain as testimony to their lives.

GERMANS IN THE POOL

Signs state, quite clearly, in Czech and German both,
That diving is forbidden, and tossing balls
Verboten, too, and so they seem uncouth

At least, as rubber bubbles smack the walls
To dribble back, and beefy bodies plunk
And souse, indifferent to our pleading calls

That they should heed the signs and cease to dunk
Themselves from pool's edge, missing children's heads
By inches, changing childish fun to funk.

But when I've finally had enough and said,
"Why can't you goddamned Germans do what's right?"
So loudly the pool grows quiet, fills with dread,

I'm sickly certain I've just picked a fight
With fourteen Huns whose bodies' total weight
Of sixteen hundred kilos will soon light

Upon my face and chest to seal my fate,
Or crush it flat, and my vacation weeks
Of snowy slopes and mountain air deflate.

I stare through soot-stained glass at creamy peaks
And watch the tiny skiers weaving down.
The heated breath inside this greenhouse reeks

Of chlorine, and from the quiet tension sound
The chugging hisses of electric pumps
That suck and filter pissed-in water round

And through a chambered cycle, and then dump
It back for healthy contact with our skin.
My German brothers rest their German rumps

Against the pool wall, cross their arms, begin
To weigh their options, maybe feel the need
To pry their horseplay from their fathers' sins.

Inciting all to make those Nazis bleed,
The propaganda flicks I grew up on
Still work their magic for this goofy breed

Of bad boys frolicking, by bargains drawn
To where their fathers' fathers once impressed
A wicked will, and now this cheerful spawn

Seems merely ancient wickedness at rest.
They smirk and wave me off and shoot me stares,
As if this were my problem more than theirs.

TICK

A rare occasion our child was not with one
Or both of us, we poked through Prague's clogged streets,
Domestic errands in our wake, until
The gray Mercedes surged to lunge ahead
Of our little red Fiesta, even though
The bottleneck of traffic halted all.
He imperiled us, almost caused a crash,
Simply to gain a length's advantage
In the stalled and stinky summer queue of cars.
Dominika slammed her palm into the horn,
Showed her teeth, and I was delighted by
Her anger, so scooted out the door and flipped
The bastard off with both my middle fingers.
He leaped out scowling and ready for a fight.
He tried to kick me but I blocked it, boxed
His ear and plucked his forehead, pointed at
His car as if he were a little boy
And I his daddy pointing to his room.
A swarthy fellow wearing pricey clothes,
He seemed a Slavic low-rent Casanova.
But when he popped his trunk and pulled out black
And shiny rags he peeled from metal, then
Snatched a cartridge and jammed it in and spun
I saw his fully automatic thing
For killing, his Uzi or whatever god
Damned thing it was, an automatic weapon,
The kind that sprays its bullets so that aiming's

Not an issue, and suddenly I thought
That here at last I'd done it. I'd finally pissed
Off someone with a weapon and the will
To use it, after years of mouthing off
In biker bars and leaning on my horn
In New Orleans—where once good men got lynched
For less—after a youth of not caring whom
I angered and well into middle life
Unscarred, unbowed, in Prague, in summer, I
Would die of road rage, but thought the noble thing
To do would be to run aslant, drawing fire
Away from Dominika, and in the tick
It took to turn I saw her raising Ema
Alone, and Ema living fatherless,
And Ema's face, and I heard Ema's voice
And clearly the greasy pimp didn't shoot
Or I'd not be writing this, but that tick,
That jagged piece of time, got packed
With self-recrimination, boundless love
For a child and her mother, for every friend
And minor enemy my life had vexed,
And even a little humor, for as
I turned I thought oh God I'm wearing drawers
With three small holes around the baggy crotch,
And every mother's admonition honked
Inside my head, as then I tripped and fell.

Prague Winter: Sonnet Stanzas for My Daughter

1.

My baby wants to know if she is more
American than Czech, to which I say
That she is what has never been before,
A perfect blending of the two, the play
Of what is best in both in one good girl.
At this she wonders why the kids at school
Call her "Americanka," even curl
Their lips in funny smiles to say it. "Fools,"
I blurt, but then sigh, "no, not fools, just kids."
They learn at supper tables that contempt
Is antidote to envy, that it rids
The small, green heart of what one dares not tempt
From shadows of the self-sought self: the sense
That all one's life is but a sad defense.

2.

But she who speaks two worlds with one quick tongue,
Who learns in Czech, but rants and drifts at home
In English so American its foam
Of effervescence is a tide that's sung
By Whitman no more so than dim-wit jock,
My dreamy girl just wants to be their friend.
For this she must, I tell her, learn to bend

The arc of her lone flight and join the flock,
But that the trick of knowing happiness
Is to find the perfect distance from us all,
A quantity that changes everyday.
Delight, my dear, in your sweet otherness
True friends you'll know when years compel you trawl
The dark tides of your mind, where wishes sway.

3.
The issue, finally, daughter, may well be
Those princesses of old Bohemia,
The ones you read about and can't but see
In movies, black-and-white, from when to be a
Female was to be princess of the State,
A beaming worker for the Greater Good.
In each it is the pouty royal's fate
To learn that peasants' wisdom is what should
Determine life of kingdom, but, of course,
The message is a muddle of traditions,
As finally princess learns to feel remorse
For being princess, marries prince, bears sons.
May power over love be your true art
When someday you are queen of someone's heart.

4.

Love child of the Velvet Revolution,
Residual passion of that passion play
In which no god of flesh was made to pay
For sins, just little men whose jobs were done,
Nine months into the sweet and sudden changes
Your life appeared, I held you in my arms,
And nothing from that moment would bring harms
To you, except that through my rage it ranges.
And now, but ten years after all those joys
Of chucking off absurdity of brutes,
And fashioning a gentler circumstance
By which the commerce of our lives alloys
Our baser aspects with what nature mutes,
In fools, you are the shine of second chance.

5.

My smart and drifty child, sometimes you stare
So vacantly I worry where you are,
And wonder what enchantment flew you there,
And by what charm you stalk the most bizarre
Scenarios you breathlessly relate
Upon emerging from your reverie.
Within the worlds you dream all threats abate
And Chance rewards each act of decency.
Yet over this glorious and wacky place
At Europe's heart a sorrow hangs like smoke.

A sixty-year-old evil leaves its trace
Even on such dreams as innocents evoke.
So self-consumed yet filled with empathy,
You're poised to bear your share of history.